The Making of
Economic Policy

Munich Lectures in Economics
Edited by Hans-Werner Sinn

The Making of Economic Policy: A Transaction-Cost Politics Perspective, by Avinash Dixit (1996)

In cooperation with the Council of the Center for Economic Studies of the University of Munich

Martin Beckmann, David F. Bradford, Gebhard Flaig, Otto Gandenberger, Franz Gehrels, Martin Hellwig, Bernd Huber, Mervyn King, John Komlos, Hans Möller, Richard Musgrave, Ray Rees, Bernd Rudolph, Agnar Sandmo, Karlhans Sauernheimer, Hans Schneeweiss, Robert Solow, Wolfgang Wiegard, Charles Wyplosz

The Making of
Economic Policy:
A Transaction-Cost
Politics Perspective

Avinash K. Dixit

CES

The MIT Press
Cambridge, Massachusetts
London, England

This book was set in Palatino by Technical Typesetting Inc., Baltimore,
Maryland.

Printed and bound in the United States of America.

Library of Congress Cataloging-in-Publication Data

Dixit, Avinash K.
  The making of economic policy : a transaction-cost politics
perspective / Avinash K. Dixit.
     p. cm. — (Munich lectures in economics)
  Includes bibliographical references and index.
  ISBN 0-262-04155-3 (hc: alk. paper), 0-262-54098-3 (pb)
  1. Economic policy. 2. Transaction costs. I. Title.
II. Series.
HD87.D59   1996
338.9—dc20   95-48264
                                                          CIP

Contents

Series Foreword

Every year the *CES* council awards a prize to an internationally renowned and innovative economist for outstanding contributions to economic research. The scholar is honored with the title "Distinguished *CES* Fellow" and is invited to give the "Munich Lectures in Economics."

The lectures are held at the Center for Economic Studies of the University of Munich. They introduce areas of recent or potential interest to a wide audience in a nontechnical way and combine theoretical depth with policy relevance.

Hans-Werner Sinn
Professor of Economics and Public Finance
Director of *CES*
University of Munich

Foreword

It is with particular pleasure that I write some words of introduction to the first volume of the Munich Lectures in Economics, and there are several reasons for this. The most important is of course that the first person to be appointed Distinguished Fellow of the Center for Economic Studies, Professor Avinash Dixit, is a most worthy recipient of this honor. Second, he is a longtime friend and sometime coauthor of mine and an economist with whose views of economics I am in very deep sympathy. And third, I am naturally delighted that the CES has asked me as a member of its Council to perform this task. I am sure that I express the views of all members of the Council in saying that the Lectures could not have got off to a better start to what we hope will be a long and distinguished series.

Avinash Dixit was born in Bombay in 1944. He holds bachelor degrees in mathematics and physics from the universities of Bombay and Cambridge and received his Ph.D. in economics from MIT in 1968. He taught at the University of California, Berkeley, Oxford University, and the University of Warwick before being appointed professor at Princeton University in 1981.

Dixit has contributed to a number of different fields in economics. He started out in the late 1960s as a development economist, producing several papers on the topic of dual economies, but he soon branched off into other fields. One of these was public economics. He was one of the early contributors to the modern development of second-best optimum tax theory, and he wrote an article on the theory of tax and price reform (*Journal of Public Economics,* 1975) that has become a modern classic. Another important area has been international economics, where among other things he wrote the book *Theory of International Trade* (1980) together with my colleague Victor Norman. He has contributed a number of important papers to the theory of industrial organization and market structure, and in recent years he has been especially active in writing about investment decisions under uncertainty, where a particularly important contribution is his book with Robert Pindyck, *Investment Under Uncertainty* (1994).

Dixit's writings are of many different types. Naturally, a large number of his publications are journal articles reporting on original research into economic theory. But he has also produced a number of surveys and interpretive article, and he has obviously enjoyed writing books; I have already referred to some of them. For completeness I should also mention his textbooks on optimization theory (1990) and growth theory (1976), and not least, his wonderful book with Barry Nalebuff on game theory, *Thinking Strategically* (1991). If you have not already read some of his books, you should immediately read the one closest to your own specialty, and then—to become a reasonably diversified economist—at least one more. I guarantee you that you will not only learn a lot, you will also enjoy yourself.

One of Dixit's most recent publications is an article called "My System of Work (Not!)" (*The American Economist,* 1994). He says in the introduction that being asked to write such an article is a clear sign of approaching senility—much like, I suppose, being asked to write a foreword to someone else's series of lectures. Be that as it may, in this article he compares types of economists with types of runners. Some, like Robert Lucas and James Mirrlees, are marathoners who stick to one research program for a decade or longer and make very basic and deep contributions to it. Others, like Hal Varian and Barry Nalebuff, are sprinters who move rapidly from one topic to another, leaving their mark on many fields of economics. Dixit's advice to young economists is "Discover your best distance." He himself is, I believe, a middle-distance runner. He is certainly not a marathoner, but he tends to run longer races than the typical sprinter. In athletics I have always felt that the best distances to watch are the 800 and 1,500 meters, and I suspect I feel the same way about economists.

It is typical of this middle-distance runner that when asked to give the Munich Lectures in Economics, he should choose a topic that strikes out in a new direction, relative to his previous work. Economists have always taken a keen interest in matters of economic policy; indeed, that interest was much of the driving force behind the development of economics as an academic discipline. Much of the writing on economic policy takes a normative approach; the emphasis is on the design of optimal policies relative to some assumption about social goals. It is only recently—over the last two or three decades—that economists have started on a systematic exploration of the positive approach to the study of economic policy, attempting to provide explanations of actual policy choices. A good deal of progress has been made, but much also remains to be done, not least on the theoretical side. It is therefore very gratifying that Avinash Dixit has decided to bring his analytical powers to bear on the theme of "The Making of Economic Policy."

Agnar Sandmo
Norwegian School of Economics
    and Business Administration
Member of CES Council

Preface

Economists usually communicate their ideas to their fellow professionals in one of two forms: articles or books. Articles focus on very specific questions, must use their scarce space for technical matters, and allow no room for any general conceptual themes or speculation. Books are for large and essentially complete bodies of research and are expected to be quite thorough and comprehensive in their scope.

The relatively rare format of a short monograph, particularly one based on a set of lectures, is a delightful halfway house for an author. One has enough space to go beyond the narrow focus of an article and to lay out some larger issues and themes but not enough to be either thorough or comprehensive. One can construct a promising framework, offer some speculative comments, and hope to arouse the readers' interest in the overall approach, without having to carry the burden of the necessity to strive for completeness or detail.

I was therefore particularly happy to have the opportunity to deliver the first of a new annual series of Munich Lectures in Economics and to develop them into this short monograph. It allowed me to pursue some ideas on political economy.

Like any theorist of international trade policy, I have been increasingly interested in the political process by which such policies are made. The reality of most countries' trade policies is so blatantly contrary to all the normative prescriptions of the economist that there is no way to understand it except by delving into the politics. Economists working in other policy-related fields, for example public finance, industrial organization, macroeconomic (fiscal and monetary) policies, and international economic conflict and coordination, have similarly perceived the need to pay attention to politics. In the other direction, political scientists have developed greater interest in economic policies, and in formal models of elections, legislation, and regulation.

In the last two decades, this integration of politics and economics has proceeded apace and has produced many different approaches and models. True to the spirit of the short monograph format, I have selectively sampled from this literature and found some themes that allow a conceptual unification of much of this literature. The first of these is the idea of "transaction costs." In economics, this has come to mean a very general class of information, negotiation, and enforcement problems that affect the internal organization of firms and the outcomes of market and nonmarket relations among firms, workers and so on. A similar and even more severe class of transaction costs pervades political relations and affects political outcomes. Many models of political economy in the literature, dealing with principal-agent problems, commitment and credibility issues, and so on can be viewed in this broad framework of "transaction-cost politics." Many features and outcomes of the policy process can be better understood and related to each other by thinking of them as the results of various transaction costs and of the strategies of the participants to cope with these costs. Second, within this general framework, a particularly important feature of the political process of making economic policy can be identified, namely, the "common agency," where several players in the political game try to influence the actions of one decisionmaker. I find that it leads to a severe diminution of the power of the incentives that can be offered to the latter; such weakness of incentives may be the key to understanding many otherwise puzzling outcomes of the political process.

At an even more basic or background level, the transaction-cost politics view leads me to argue that the political process should be viewed as indeed a *process*—taking place in real time, governed and constrained by history, and containing surprises for all parties. In this view, the traditional dichotomy of markets versus governments, and the question of which system performs better, largely lose their relevance. Markets and governments are both facts of economic life, and they interact in complex ways. We cannot find feasible improvements by wishing away one of the components. For example, economists cannot claim that market failures can be corrected simply by showing that the optimal outcome in a model of a social-welfare maximizing entity divorced from any real political process will outperform the market. The most we can do is to understand how the combined economic-political system evolves mechanisms to cope with the variety of transaction costs that it must face.

The short monograph format proved very suitable for exploring these ideas, but it has its limitations. The analysis and the conclusions must remain very preliminary and suggestive. But I hope that they will interest or provoke future researchers of the political process of economic policymaking, and will lead to more technical article-type research as well as more comprehensive book-type products. A monograph with a mixed potential readership—professional economists, political scientists, and policy practitioners—must contain some unevenness of exposition. I thought it necessary to give brief explanations of some very basic concepts like credibility, and of some simple properties of incentive schemes; economists and political scientists familiar with the literature may find this unnecessary. I also go into some details of the literature, including in one case a technical appendix; some practitioners may find this material incomprehensible or regard it as irrelevant. Let me apologize to both these groups in advance.

It is a pleasure to thank everyone who helped me in this endeavor. Most important, I am very grateful to the Center for Economic Studies at the University of Munich, and its director, Professor Hans-Werner Sinn, for inviting me to give the first Munich Lectures in Economics and thereby giving me an opportunity to engage in this very interesting and stimulating line of reading and thinking. I also thank the other faculty and staff at the Center, particularly Christian Thimann, for their hospitality during the week I visited them and gave the lectures.

Several individuals discussed the ideas with me at the early stages, pointed out to me some pertinent literature, and read and commented on previous versions of the manuscript. Among them, David Bradford and Bengt Holmström deserve special mention. I also received very valuable criticism, advice, and suggestions from Giuseppe Bertola, Timothy Besley, James Buchanan, Peter Diamond, Paul Joskow, Meir Kohn, Anne Krueger, John Londregan, Douglass North, Mancur Olson, Dani Rodrik, Thomas

Romer, Hans-Werner Sinn, Robert Solow, Pablo Spiller, Christian Thimann, Jean Tirole, Oliver Williamson, Richard Zeckhauser, and three anonymous readers for The MIT Press. These are real experts in many aspects of the subject that I was exploring tentatively as a beginner; therefore, I am particularly grateful for their willingness to share their insights. However, this is a topic so conducive to disagreements and controversy that I should emphasize that I remain solely responsible for the final product.

Avinash K. Dixit

1   Economic Policymaking as a Political Process

When economists and other analysts of public affairs think about economic policy, they often pose the basic question as a confrontation between markets and governments. On the one side are those who believe that markets are prone to failures, that governments emerge to correct the failures of markets, and that on the whole they are capable of doing so. On the other side, we find those who believe that markets perform well and that governments are the problem, not the solution.

As usual, reality is much more complex and defeats any attempts to fit it into such neat dichotomies. Markets have their flaws, as do governments, and observers and analysts of the two systems have their own limitations. Herbert Stein, who has over 50 years of experience as an economist in the political world of Washington, D.C., summarized what he had learned in two main lessons: "Economists do not know very much [about the economy]; other people, including the politicians who make economic policy, know even less" (quoted in Hamilton, 1992, p. 62). Alan Blinder, who combines first-rate skills and reputation as an academic economist and policy practitioner, has given us a "Murphy's law" of economic policy: "Economists have the

least influence on policy where they know the most and
are most agreed; they have the most influence on policy
where they know the least and disagree most vehemently."
(Blinder 1987, p. 1)

In this short monograph, based on three lectures delivered at the University of Munich, I will attempt to bring
a fresh perspective to the issues of economic policymaking and their analysis. My status is very much that of an
outsider, and a theorist rather than a practitioner, but this
has its advantages. One can remain detached from the fray
and from the ideological attachment that affects the thinking of many of the more active participants. Therefore, one
can better balance the strengths and the weaknesses of the
conflicting arguments, spot common ground where the an-
tagonists might fail to detect it, and attempt to evolve a
more broadly acceptable synthesis. Moreover, a "middle-
brow" theorist like me can try to relate the applied and
historical literature to some abstractly theoretical models.

My starting points are simple to the point of being trite—
one must accept that markets and governments are both
imperfect systems; that both are unavoidable features of
reality; that the operation of each is powerfully influenced
by the existence of the other; and that both are processes
unfolding in real time, whose evolution is dependent on
history and buffeted by surprises. Most important, I will
argue that the political process should be viewed as a game
between many participants (principals) who try to affect
the actions of the immediate policymaker (agent). What follows from these observations is orthogonal to, and perhaps
destructive of, the whole "markets versus governments"
debate. The equilibrium or the outcome of the game of
policymaking will typically not maximize anything. Any

attempts to design, or even identify the desiderata of, a truly optimal system are doomed to failure, and no grand or general results about the superiority of one organizational form over another can be expected. What we can do is to understand how the whole system consisting of markets and governments copes with the whole set of problems of conflicting information, incentives, and actions that preclude a fully ideal outcome. What I offer is a structure or a framework that can help our thinking about several specific issues of economic policymaking, and occasionally, help us identify some specific points for beneficial intervention.

Of course I hold no expectation of settling any debates. The issues are too large and too complex, and the format of a short monograph based on three lectures is too brief to permit more than a mere beginning of an agenda of research. I hope that the statement of such an agenda will stimulate some readers to investigate my suggestions and examine whether or how far they stand up to more specific and detailed modeling.

In this chapter, I offer a brief review of the two main alternatives that have dominated economic policy analysis during the last five decades, and suggest a synthesis, labeled "transaction-cost politics," that views policymaking as a process in real time. In the next chapter, I develop this idea further, and attempt to place some recent literature on political economy within its scope. In chapter 3, I will illustrate the transaction-cost politics approach using the vehicle of two case studies, which briefly examine particular policy issues and organizations in its light. Some of the earlier conceptual discussion will look ahead to these case studies and use their findings to illustrate the points being made.

1.1 The Normative Approach to Policy Analysis

Much of the theory, and almost all of the practice, of economic policy analysis views the making and implementation of the policy as a technical problem, even as a control engineering problem. One starts with a model of the workings of the economy, along with some degrees of freedom, or some instruments of policy intervention. Then one assumes an evaluation criterion. Finally, one calculates the values of the instruments that will maximize the criterion, or directions of change that will improve the performance as judged by the criterion. These policy choices, or reforms, are to be recommended to the government, or offered in public discussions, as the right ones.

The specification of the economic models, policy instruments, and evaluation criteria varies greatly in different applications. It also varies across countries. Our understanding of the issues involved in specifying models of the economy has improved greatly as a result of cumulative research over time, but the above description of the method of policy analysis retains its general validity.

At the level of pure theory, the evaluation criterion is almost always some form of the Bergson-Samuelson welfare function, expressing social welfare as an increasing function of individual utilities. In practice, several proxies may be applied. In microeconomic applications, consumer and producer surpluses capture aggregate economic welfare with some accuracy, and distributional considerations are often added on in an ad hoc manner. In macroeconomics the proxies are even more indirect. Employment or unemployment serve as rough measures of both the current aggregate welfare and its distribution in one particular dimension; inflation gives some idea of intertemporal tradeoffs, and so on. But some thought of a familiar welfare function can be said to lurk behind all these practices.[1]

In its earliest uses, the Bergson-Samuelson function was maximized subject only to the economy's resource and technology constraints, as if the government could choose all the activities of all the firms and all the choices of all the consumers. This was termed the "first-best," and the second theorem of welfare economics proved that it could be implemented using a set of competitive and complete markets once the initial ownership of resources was suitably allocated. This established a link between policy analysis in the Bergson-Samuelson tradition on the one hand, and the positive competitive equilibrium theory, which began with Walras and culminated with Arrow and Debreu, on the other hand.

In other words, this line of thinking established that perfect markets and perfect governments do an equally good job of achieving economic efficiency. The role of a perfect government was therefore interpreted as that of correcting market failures—using Pigovian taxes or subsidies to replace missing markets or correct externalities, providing public goods, and achieving an ethically desirable distribution of resources. These ideas also provided the basis for the advocacy of the welfare state especially in the Scandinavian countries; see Sandmo (1991, sections 4, 5) for an excellent review and discussion.

In one sense, this forms the basis for a *positive* theory of government. According to this view, the government's role in the economy emerges and evolves to perform those

---

1. Some stop short of specifying a welfare function and merely characterize the entire Pareto frontier under the assumed constraints on instruments, contracts, or information. These are not by themselves entire policy analyses but intermediate steps which must then be completed using further arguments which can be of either normative or positive kinds.

economic functions that markets cannot handle, or at least cannot perform well. In public finance, the view of government as the remedy for market failures is probably best remembered from Musgrave's (1959) three-way classification of the objectives and the administration of fiscal policy and the budget: allocation, concerned with the provision of public goods and services, correction of externalities, and so on; distribution, concerned with taxes and transfers to achieve a more just distribution of income or wealth; and stabilization, or maintenance of a high but noninflationary level of aggregate demand and employment in the economy. This view lies behind much of the development of public economics in the 1960s and 1970s. In industrial economics, there is a similar tradition of "public interest" theories of regulation that view policy as a response to monopoly and other market failures; see Noll (1989, section 2) for an excellent exposition and discussion of these. At an even more basic level, this approach can be traced back to Hobbes, who viewed the government as a social contract that enables people to escape from the "state of nature" where their competition in pursuit of self-interest would lead to a destructive "war of all against all" (Russell 1945, pp. 550–551).

However, this tradition did not go on to provide any positive theory of how the government would *function* after its formation. It simply assumed that the government would maximize social welfare, and therefore in its operational content the theory remained normative. Indeed, Musgrave himself said that his concern was "primarily with the ... normative view" (1959, p. 4).

Over time, the normative approach to policy has been greatly enriched in its treatment of the underlying model of the economy. Even though the ideas and their history are now well known, to the point that detailed citations are unnecessary, I shall offer a very cursory review to set the stage for the discussion of alternative approaches. Policy analysis was soon modified to include additional constraints on the government's actions. If some of the conditions of optimality in the first-best could not be met, then the constrained optimum, or the second-best, would typically require an appropriately tailored violation of the remaining conditions. This possibility, first pointed out in this general form by Lipsey and Lancaster, was soon examined in many specific contexts, and appropriate second-best responses were analyzed. The work of Boiteux on optimal departures from marginal cost pricing in regulated industries, and that of Bhagwati, Ramaswami, Srinivasan, Johnson, and others on the hierarchy of domestic and trade policies to correct externalities and meet noneconomic constraints, are important instances of these developments.

In public finance, the focus was on optimal uses of limited tax instruments available to the government. The role of commodity taxes in achieving efficiency and distributional objectives when personalized lump-sum transfers were not available was clarified by the seminal work of Diamond and Mirrlees. Baumol and Bradford also related this analysis to that of optimal pricing mentioned above.

The next important development was the recognition of informational limitations on the policymakers. Here, the start came from Mirrlees' work on the income tax. His method was used by Spence and others for analyzing nonlinear pricing. This line of research on the design of incentive-compatible planning mechanisms has now culminated in the impressive work of Laffont and Tirole (1993) on regulation, and Guesnerie (1995) on taxation. The corresponding evolution in economists' thinking about practical aspects of policy in the welfare state is discussed by Sandmo (1991, section 7).

The importance of informational limitations on the workings of the economy, and on the potential for improving matters through policy intervention, has been impressed upon the profession with the greatest emphasis and clarity by the work of Stiglitz. His recent statements (1989, p. 38; 1994, p. 28) are particularly noteworthy. He invokes his work with Greenwald (1986), establishing that market equilibria with imperfect or incomplete information are generally not constrained Pareto efficient; a government subject to the same informational limitations can achieve better outcomes. For Stiglitz, this is the central proposition that establishes the presumptive merit of policy activism, and much of his policy analysis flows from it.

Impressive as these achievements are, they assume a single social-welfare-maximizing principal and thereby leave out a crucial aspect of economic policymaking, namely, the political process. As a crude but effective caricature, one can say that normative policy analysis began by supposing that the policy was made by an omnipotent, omniscient, and benevolent dictator. The work on the second-best removed the omnipotence. That on information removed the omniscience. However, the assumptions of benevolence and dictatorship have remained unaffected by all these improvements in our understanding of the limits on instruments and information. This fits well with the Hobbesian lineage and spirit of this approach, which were noted above. Hobbes's favored form of government was the monarchy, or at least the supreme central authority of the commonwealth or the Leviathan (see Russell 1945, p. 551). The normative approach continues to view policymaking as a purely *technical* problem. The implicit assumption is that once a policy that maximizes or improves social welfare has been found and recommended, it will be implemented as designed, and the desired effects will follow.

In reality, a policy proposal is merely the beginning of a process that is *political* at every stage—not merely the process of legislation, but also the implementation, including the choice or formation of an administrative agency and the subsequent operation of this agency. The standard normative approach to policy analysis views this whole process as a social-welfare-maximizing black box, exactly as the neoclassical theory of production and supply viewed the firm as a profit-maximizing black box. While some useful insights follow from this, it leaves some very important gaps in our understanding and gives us some very misleading ideas about the possibilities of beneficial policy intervention. Economists studying business and industrial organization have long recognized the inadequacy of the neoclassical view of the firm and have developed richer paradigms and models based on the concepts of various kinds of transactions costs. Policy analysis also stands to benefit from such an approach, opening the black box and examining the actual workings of the mechanism inside. That is the starting point, and a recurrent theme, of this monograph.

The theorists who developed the normative approach are not unaware of the political process. Thus Stiglitz (1989, p. 45; 1994, p. 32) cautions us that there are "political failures" just as there are market failures, that they are often rooted in the same informational problems, and that the potential for beneficial policy activism that follows from the Greenwald-Stiglitz theorem may not actually materialize. But the relative emphasis given to market failures and

political failures in his writings makes it abundantly clear
where he judges the balance to be—in favor of the government and against the market. The implicit belief that comes
through is that political failures can be avoided through
good management, namely, by giving power to make and
implement economic policy to an economist, presumably
(preferably?) to Stiglitz himself.[2]
Practitioners and policy advisers know that the reality
of economic policy is very far from the picture Stiglitz
paints. Neither Stiglitz nor any other economist has the
powers of a benevolent (although no longer either omnipotent nor omniscient) dictator.[3] The political process of
economic policymaking is constantly influenced by the legislature, the executive and its agencies, the courts, various
special-interest lobbies, the media, and so on. The legislature may fail to enact the economist's desired policies; the
administrative process may fail to implement the legislated
policies in the intended manner. The outcomes may fail
to correct market failures and may instead introduce new
costs of their own.
Some models in the theory of information and incentives make some allowance for politics by stipulating that
the government has an objective function with different
weights attached to the welfare of different groups of income recipients. The weights are intended to reflect their
different political powers. This is an important step in the
right direction, but it falls short of being a complete model
of the political process, whose essence is that many partici-

---

2. Some of the discussants of Stiglitz's essay (1989), most notably North
and Bös, also point out the importance of political and institutional
processes.
3. Since this was written, Stiglitz has become Chairman of President Clinton's Council of Economic Advisers. I believe my assertion remains valid.

pants simultaneously try to influence the actions of the immediate policymaker. The equilibrium of this game of strategy needs to be modeled; it may not maximize anything. Some very recent literature shows some recognition of this, for example, Tirole (1994) mentions the issue, and Laffont and Tirole (1993, chapters 11, 15–16) model some political games of industry regulation, but only Wilson (1989) and Grossman and Helpman (1994) have made the existence of multiple principals (common agency) a central concern. I will argue in chapter 2 that many important features of the political process, such as the weakness of incentives and the economically inefficient outcomes, can be attributed to this cause.

Nowhere is the economic inefficiency and waste of actual policies more apparent than in the area of international trade. Workers and other stakeholders in industries that are adversely affected by foreign competition are often protected by import quotas, price supports, and so on. There are reasons of equity and reasons of political reality that would lead many policy advisers to favor some help or support for these groups, but economists would advocate more direct transfers or retraining grants for this purpose. The instruments that are used in practice, typically tariffs and quotas, cause a great deal of unnecessary economic harm. In the United States, for example, the cost to consumers of saving one job in an industry suffering from import competition typically runs into six figures, several times the wage of the worker (see Hufbauer, Berliner, and Elliott 1986; Hufbauer and Elliott 1994). Observers of this phenomenon, for example Krueger (1990), have recognized politics as the force behind these outcomes. They have even made some tentative suggestions for the design of policy; for example, they favor transparency.

Formal modeling of the political process of economic policymaking has made significant progress in some areas. The Stigler-Peltzman "capture" theory of regulation is an early example; the last decade has seen important advances in positive theories of macroeconomic (fiscal and monetary) policies and international policy conflict and coordination. I briefly discuss some of this research in the next chapter. However, more general recognition of the political process in economic policy analysis is urgently needed. In the meantime, many practitioners continue to operate in the normative mode. Those who support policy activism argue in terms of the benefits that *would* be available *if* their favored policies were implemented without any modification or leakage in the political process. These benefits are not likely to be realized when the policy recommendations are filtered through the political process. Those on the opposite side of the policy debates argue that the government *should not* interfere with the markets, either because they believe that the markets perform well, or because they believe that political failures are even worse than market failures, but they are being equally unrealistic. There is no such thing as deciding to leave things to markets and leaving them— governments will continue to have the power to intervene in the economy and will continue to use it. Indeed, experience shows that most right-wing governments intervene in the economy just as much as do left-wing ones, albeit in somewhat different directions. For example, the Reagan administration always claimed to be a very strong proponent of free trade but initiated and implemented several protectionist measures, such as the renewal and tightening of the Multi-Fiber Arrangement (MFA), the "voluntary" restraints on Japanese auto exports to the United States, and the import quotas on steel, motorcycles, and so on.

1.2   The Positive View of Political Economy

The best-known alternative to normative policy analysis is the *public choice* or *contractarian* framework, long championed by Buchanan and others. Buchanan and Tullock (1962) gave the first detailed statement of this approach, and recent clarifications, elaborations, and restatements can be found in Buchanan (1975, 1987, and 1988). Buchanan emphasizes the distinction between the constitution that governs the whole policy process and individual instances of policymaking within this constitution. The distinction is also reminiscent of Lucas's distinction between a policy regime and a policy action on a specific occasion within the regime. The outcome of any particular policymaking exercise, which I shall call a *policy act* for brevity, is determined, for Buchanan, by the working of the process within the rules that were laid down. At this stage there are no degrees of freedom, so normative analysis is irrelevant. " 'That which emerges' is 'that which emerges' and that is that" (Buchanan 1975, p. 226).

For Buchanan, normative judgments are appropriate when the underlying *constitution* of policy, that is, the set of rules that will govern the making of individual policy acts, is being determined. Improvements should be sought in the rules of the game. Indeed, he goes further and argues that such reforms should, and perhaps more important, can, be made on the basis of unanimity. Everyone knows that the constitution under discussion will continue to set the rules of the game for a long time to come. One's own economic future over this horizon is very uncertain. Therefore one is placed "behind a partial 'veil of uncertainty' concerning the effects of any rule on his own predicted interest," and the choice among rules will "tend to be based on generalizable criteria of fairness." One may "rationally prefer a rule that will, on particular occasions, operate to produce results that are opposed to his own interests," so long as "on balance, over the whole sequence of 'plays,' his own interests [are] more effectively served" by the rule. (Buchanan 1987, p. 248).

Rawls (1971) has a similar theme, and by making a specific assumption about individual preferences, arrives at a definite and quite extreme rule. If individuals are very risk-averse, then they will agree on a rule that, when the ignorance is lifted, will maximize the well-being of the worst-off member of society (maxi-min). Harsanyi (1953) makes a less extreme assumption about risk-aversion, namely, that every individual behind the veil of ignorance has the same von Neumann-Morgenstern expected utility function. Then each one, regarding oneself equally likely to end up in any one of the possible specific identities, wants the social welfare function to be the equal-weight average or the sum of all utilities; this means unanimous agreement in favor of utilitarianism.

The comparison with Rawls also brings out a different aspect of Buchanan's approach, which was more explicit in that of his precursor, Wicksell (1896). Rawls regards his idea of the maxi-min contract made behind the veil of ignorance as a theory of justice. Likewise, for Wicksell the contractarian approach was the basis for a *just procedure*. This is to be contrasted with the idea of *just outcomes* that is often taken by the normative social-welfare-maximizing economists. In this sense, the Wicksell-Buchanan approach also has a normative aspect, but it deals in judgments about the justness of the contract or the constitution.

The same applies a fortiori to the question of efficiency. In the contractarian view, there is no such thing as a judgment of efficiency or inefficiency concerning individual policy acts. The efficiency of a constitution should be judged in the light of its likely effect over its whole lifetime, averaged over all the policy acts in varied contexts and instances where it might be applied. In fact Buchanan's judgment on existing constitutions seems even more cautiously applied. He asks: "Could the observed rules that constrain the activity of ordinary politics have emerged from agreement in constitutional contract?" And he is willing to offer a clear answer in the negative for only one case: that of fiscal deficits. "It is almost impossible to construct a contractual calculus in which representatives of separate generations would agree to allow majorities in a single generation to finance currently enjoyed public consumption through the issue of public debt" (Buchanan 1987, pp. 249–50).[4]

Buchanan's writings have been very influential among thinkers on economic policy matters, especially in Europe. Formal work along these lines has focused on issues of credibility and the benefit from making commitments to particular rules and organizations. Constitutions are, then, the method of making the commitments credible. This line of thinking is probably most developed for macroeconomic fiscal and monetary policies, for example, the independence of the central bank. This research is discussed by Persson and Tabellini (1990), and many of the original articles are collected in Persson and Tabellini 1994a. There is also some recent formal work on these lines in the theory of regulation of industries and public utilities, for example, Laffont and Tirole 1993, parts V and VI.

---

4. As Eisner and others have emphasized, some current public expenditure may be an investment; more on this later.

The public choice approach is recognized as being important in its emphasis on the political process, but on the whole, it appears that the normative mode continues to command broader support. Much of actual policy analysis, whether in theoretical modeling, quantification, or public discussion, continues to evaluate individual policy acts in normative terms. What might be the reasons for this divergence? I can think of several.

First, one must recognize the possibility that many economists find Buchanan's views unpalatable because their triumph would leave economists with little to do. Constitutional reforms are on the agenda only on rare and infrequent occasions. In the meantime, economists would be reduced to descriptive research on the workings of the economy and of the policy process, and to the frankly partisan task of advising their side in this process how it can best play the game. Economists can earn more income by acting as consultants who offer better policies, and more professional prestige by offering objective prescriptions to achieve greater efficiency in the interests of all. Therefore, even if Buchanan is right, economists might do best to pretend that normatively guided policy intervention is possible on individual occasions, and to claim that they have the right disinterested expertise for the purpose.

The second possibility is that general ideas by themselves are not enough to carry the day in modern scientific discourse; they must be supported by more concrete or formal models. Only thus can one draw the full set of implications from a theory and test them against observation or intuition. There are numerous instances where ideas languished until modeling techniques developed that could handle the ideas and explore their consequences. The importance of increasing returns and complementarities in the process of economic development was recognized from the earliest stages of economists' thinking about the subject. But a lack of acceptable models kept these ideas in the background for three decades, while attention focused on the more tractable issues of capital accumulation with constant or diminishing returns. Only recently have growth models with imperfect competition and external economies allowed economists to understand the process of development in richer detail. Similarly, formal models of the contractarian approach in action in specific contexts have been slow to develop.

In saying this, I do not mean to fault economists for being dazzled by formal models and blind to the value of more loosely expressed ideas. On the contrary, I regard formal modeling as an important part of the scrutiny of ideas. It is too easy to be convinced by verbal arguments where assumptions are not spelled out, and additional and possibly contradictory implications are not fully investigated. We are right to adopt a wary attitude, but we should also be eager to develop formal models of intriguing and potentially important ideas and hypotheses. Good ideas shine far more brightly when supported by good models.[5]

In its early years, the public choice approach to economic policy may have suffered from the relative scarcity of good models of the political process of policymaking. The normative approach came ready equipped with an elegant formal apparatus, which facilitated the development of models elaborating its foundations. By contrast, the public choice approach initially consisted of a concept, lacking a general organizing formalism, and specific models

---

5. See Krugman (1994) for a discussion of the recent history of thought in development economics and a similar conclusion about the role of formal models.

were slow to develop. If this is the real reason for its relative neglect, however, the future should be bright, because the last decade or more has brought rapid and substantial progress. Mueller (1989) reviewed the state of the art in public finance at the time of his writing. Macroeconomic policy analysis has gone farthest with important work on dynamic policy games of commitment and credibility; this was reviewed and collected in Persson and Tabellini 1994a, b. Such models give us just the right apparatus with which Buchanan's distinction between constitutions and policy acts can be developed and explored in more detail.

A third possible reason for the relative lack of popularity of Buchanan's ideas among many economists may be that they do not like the results of many positive analyses of political economy. Observers of the political equilibria that lead to policy acts often argue that policy does more harm than good. Such is the finding of the "regulatory capture" theorists in industrial organization (see the review and discussion in Noll 1989, section 3). Many economists who were drawn to the subject with the intention of helping to design policies that would improve the economic conditions find this unpalatable. At the basic level, however, the public choice approach merely insists on the recognition of the constitutional framework and political institutions in the economist's study of policy, with no presumption about, and indeed no encouragement to pass, any normative judgments on policy acts. In other contexts, or once all the appropriate constraints on information and action are taken into account, the analysis may show that the system does quite a creditable job of coping with the problems. I will have more to say on this in chapter 2, and will offer some remarks about economists' role in the policy process in chapter 4.

Finally, a fourth reason for economists' hesitancy in accepting the public choice approach may be that its distinction between the constitution of economic policy and the policy process in individual instances is too sharply drawn to be realistic. Although policy rules and acts are useful pure or idealized conceptual categories to focus our thought, in reality the distinction between them is more gradual, and there are some degrees of freedom for intervention at almost all points. This leads to a synthesis of the normative and positive approaches, which requires us to take the history and the institutions of politics seriously but also permits useful economic input of various kinds. In the next section I will discuss these claims in greater detail.

1.3   A Synthesis: The Policy Process in "Real Time"

The distinction between a constitution for economic policy and individual policy acts is blurred in reality because each aspect encroaches on the other to a significant extent. Of course the designer of a constitution should look ahead and examine what acts it will lead to in various future circumstances, and use this knowledge to achieve an optimal design. This is essentially a "backward induction" or "subgame perfectness" argument (see Diamond 1994); but I mean something more. A constitution never lays down the clear, firm, and comprehensive set of rules that the contractarian approach depicts, so there is room for maneuver in individual acts. Conversely, many policy acts can have long-lasting consequences akin to rules. I will now state several reasons for this blurring of the distinction, and illustrate them using examples, often looking ahead to the two case studies that will form the topic of the third chapter.

Constitutions Are Incomplete Contracts

If constitutions are contracts, they are very incomplete ones. They do not spell out the rules and procedures to be followed in every conceivable instance in precise detail. They leave much to be interpreted and determined in specific future eventualities. The reasons for this are basically the same as the reasons why most business contracts are incomplete, namely, (1) the inability to foresee all the possible contingencies, (2) the complexity of specifying rules, even for the numerous contingencies that can be foreseen, and (3) the difficulty of objectively observing and verifying contingencies so that the specified procedures may be put into action.[6] All these problems are even more important in the case of policy constitutions than they are for business contracts. Constitutions last much longer than most business relationships. Economic circumstances change radically during the life of a constitution, both for cyclical and secular reasons. Business contracts are at least confined to the provision of a particular good or service; economywide changes are much more dramatic. Conflicts and disagreements about contingencies are much more common in the political arena than in business. A constitution of economic policy has to be couched in sufficiently general terms that it can be interpreted and applied as the economy itself changes in dramatic and unpredictable ways.

In this process of interpretation and application, there can be very large variations in the way a given rule op-

---

6. See Williamson 1985 for a detailed discussion of these issues. Barzel (1989, especially chapter 5) emphasizes that property rights are always imprecisely delineated for similar sets of reasons and examines the workings of markets and other contractual arrangements in this light.

erates. These variations naturally occur in response to the political realities of the time. In other words, an incomplete constitution can be manipulated by the participants to serve their own aims. Some examples will help make the point.

The United States' Constitution gives the Congress the responsibility for the federal taxes and expenditures but leaves it almost total procedural freedom in carrying out these duties. Cogan (1994) has found that procedural changes have had large impacts on budget deficits. Appropriation authority was dispersed among several congressional committees between 1880 and 1920. During this period the expenditures swelled. The authority was consolidated in a single committee of each house in the 1920s, when the expenditure was brought under control. The dispersion has increased gradually once again since the 1930s, and attempts at consolidation have had little success, even though expenditure growth is recognized to be a problem. The reason should be obvious to any economist: no one committee in a decentralized structure will internalize the overall budget constraint, and the result will be a Prisoners' Dilemma of overspending. Indeed, the problem was recognized at the time the procedural changes were being debated, but the changes were made anyway in response to the political imperatives of each era.

The General Agreement on Tariffs and Trade (GATT) was an international organization with some powers of persuasion but relatively little effective enforcement powers. When major countries or blocs found their interests conflicting with GATT's constitutional rules, they usually circumvented or simply violated the rules. GATT was generally forced to recognize the reality of the countries' political power and accommodate the trade restrictions in its structure and practices. The most important "exception" of this kind has been the Multi-Fiber Arrangement (MFA), a complex scheme of bilaterally and minilaterally (that is, within groups of a few countries) organized quotas on trade in textiles and garments. It violates almost every precept that was held to be basic in GATT's constitution—multilateralism in negotiation, equal treatment of all trading partners, and a general presumption against quantitative restrictions on trade—but the political power of the interested parties, and the momentum of the arrangement itself, combined to produce a complex system that has lasted more than three decades. The United States started a bilateral "voluntary" restraint arrangement in cotton textiles with Japan in the mid-1950s, the European countries soon joined in, and other fabrics and countries were added as the protective purposes of the original agreements were seen to be eroded by a process of substitution. The preamble to the arrangement, and the rhetoric every time it was renewed, spoke of expanding world trade in textiles and garments, but the specifics worked exactly to the contrary purpose. In the Uruguay Round agreements it was decided that the World Trade Organization (WTO) that was established as a part of the agreement would phase out the MFA over the next decade. It remains to be seen whether and how well that resolve translates into actual outcomes; the early indications are not good.

Finally, a policy rule and institution created for one purpose can gradually acquire its own life and get transformed for quite different purposes. Krueger (1990) shows how such a transformation occurred in the U.S. sugar program in very large and unexpected ways; in chapter 3 my look at the GATT will reveal some very similar effects.

Constitutions Are Not Made Behind a Veil of Ignorance

Writers of constitutions or rules expect them to last a long time, but they are also aware that they themselves will be affected primarily by the first few years of the new constitution and its institutions and will bear any costs of transition to it. (Of course, they discount the far-off and unknown future as compared to the immediate and known future.) They are not really behind a Rawlsian veil of ignorance. For example, the framers of the U.S. Constitution were supposedly very aware that they were laying down a structure of government that would have to cope with changing times and fallible humans and therefore created the elaborate system of checks and balances that continues to operate after two centuries. But they were equally aware of their own interests. The handling of slavery in the document, and the prohibition of export taxes, reflected the politics of the time, not Buchanan's "generalizable criteria of fairness" that would command universal consent.[7]

Other instances provide even clearer support for my point. One reason the consumption tax has failed to replace the income tax is the transition costs that some people will have to bear. When the GATT was being formed in the years just after World War II, each of the major powers had special interests and arrangements they wanted to protect. Britain and France had their imperial connections; these were "grandfathered" into the GATT even though they violated the principle of equal treatment of all trading partners (the "most favored nation" or MFN

---

7. Alas, the Southern exporting interests who insisted that the Constitution should forbid export taxes were unaware of "Lerner symmetry" and failed to win a similar provision of no import restrictions.

principle). In the recent Uruguay Round leading to the new World Trade Organization (WTO), all the parties had very definite interests they wanted to protect. The United States was under no doubt as to whether it would be an importer or an exporter of clothing in any foreseeable future. European farmers had no expectation that theirs would become a booming industry that would compete on level terms with those in Australia or Canada. And the less-developed countries knew that they would be net users, not producers, of intellectual property rights, at least for the first couple of decades of the WTO. The agreement that emerged clearly reflects these specific concerns and the political power of the groups holding these concerns, not general principles of fairness in trade. As North (1994, pp. 360–361) expressed it, "Institutions are not necessarily or even usually created to be socially efficient; rather they, or at least the formal rules, are created to serve the interests of those with the bargaining power to create new rules."

It may be useful to draw a distinction between two functions of constitutions, setting specific rules for future actions, and laying down dispute-settlement procedures that are to be followed when faced with situations that are not covered by the rules. My observations apply with particular force to the first function; the drafters of the constitution have very clear stakes in specific substantive areas. The second function, however, may be more amenable to constitutional treatment. As in the theory of the firm, it is tantamount to specifying residual rights of control or asset ownership, and there are sometimes good and commonly acceptable efficiency reasons for assigning these rights in particular ways.

Policy Acts Have Long-Lasting Effects

Individual policy acts that are made within a given set of rules may seem easy to reverse within the same framework, but they often create facts, institutions, and expectations that have their own momentum and acquire at least some of the same durability as a change in the constitution itself. Reversal becomes politically and economically costly, and there is a "hysteresis" of policy acts.

The problem is at its most severe when a policy act entails the creation of a new agency to implement it. Wilson (1989, pp. 64, 222, and others) gives an excellent account and analysis of the process. When a new agency is formed, it is given a clear task. The initial staff have some belief in the task and may indeed be self-selected for this belief. This creates an organizational culture and a sense of mission. If circumstances and the needs of policy change later, this culture becomes a barrier to change. Agencies accept innovations that improve their ability to perform the existing and accepted tasks, but changing the tasks in any significant way, or reducing the autonomy of the agency in carrying them out, is fiercely resisted. Wilson's examples range from the introduction of aircraft carriers in the United States Navy, to the addition of administering disability insurance to the United States Social Security Administration's tasks, to the use of computers in businesses as well as government agencies.

The difficulties that most former communist countries have encountered on the path of reform can be attributed to just such resistance by long-established agencies whose tasks have changed. The experience has also shown the variety and the power of the strategies and tactics that are available to government agencies for this purpose. For example, managers of collective farms, who retained control over fertilizer allocation and harvesting machinery, could stifle the attempts of individuals to start private farming by denying them access to these things at crucial times in the crop season. This example, while making the main point that policy acts cast long shadows, also helps make the reverse point: constitutional reform, or a change in the rules, often fails to make the complete break with the past that one would hope for. North (1994, p. 366) makes a similar observation with regard to the inertia of informal social norms: "[R]evolutionary change is never as revolutionary as its supporters desire."

More generally, policy acts shape the future environment by creating constituencies that gain from the policy, who will then fiercely resist any changes that take away these gains. Prominent examples are urban rent controls that benefit existing tenants, farm price supports that benefit existing farmers, and trade barriers that benefit incumbent domestic producers. In all these cases, the group is given some economic advantage or profit and is protected from new entry. Therefore the group has a particularly strong motive to form a coalition to lobby for the continuation of the policy. Then the policy can persist for a long time and despite the large cost it inflicts on the rest of the economy. Government bureaucracies have their own organizational motives to protect themselves and have very good political weapons to do so, enabling them to outlive their usefulness by years or even decades.

There is even a normative concept that defends continuance of long-standing policies even when they are inefficient. This is called the "reliance doctrine." It says that when people have made commitments (sunk investments) in the expectation of continuation of a given policy, those expectations should not be disappointed, and the resource costs they incurred in making these investments should not be rendered worthless, save for some really important offsetting reason. As more people make such sunk investments, changing a policy act becomes ever harder with the passage of time. For some, the ethical importance of a government keeping its word may be enough to justify the reliance doctrine. There is also an efficiency argument. The perception that the government will not arbitrarily change policies in the future to expropriate assets may be important to ensure that long-lived investments will be made now (see Buchanan 1988, p. 138). The reliance doctrine then becomes the way the government establishes such a reputation and credibility for its promise of nonexpropriation. For such reasons, most legislatures and courts are very wary of upsetting long-held expectations.

At a constitution-making level, the normative question of whether to incorporate the reliance doctrine will have to be answered by balancing the commitment or reputation advantages against the costs of persisting with bad outcomes on some occasions. Here my point is positive rather than normative; the doctrine makes policy acts durable and blurs the distinction between them and constitutional rules.

Inertia even thwarts constitutional reform as a whole. This is largely because constitutions cover several aspects of economic and social policy, and different groups have different views about the desirability of altering different aspects. Then each group hesitates to initiate the process of change, for the fear that this would "open up a whole can of worms" and lead to other changes that it does not want. A dramatic example of this comes from the observation that many movements that want to amend the United States Constitution for some specific purpose, for example an equal rights amendment, are unwilling to call for a constitutional convention, which might then take up many other issues that this group opposes. They would rather let their cause die. Another instance is the recent failure of the United Nations to disband the Trusteeship Council, even though its function has ended. The Council is written in the United Nations' charter, so it can only be disbanded by amending that; but once the charter is opened up, there is a risk that contending factions in various countries will destroy other valuable aspects of it. So the Council lives on. Thus, sometimes, constitutions may prove even more rigid and unchangeable than most contractarians would wish.

The idea of "path-dependence," that small changes can have long-lasting effects, and that history matters, has gained wide popularity, following the work of David (1985), Arthur (1994), and others. It is often labeled "the economics of QWERTY," because of the prevalence of the standard English typewriter keyboard long after its initial purpose became irrelevant, and notwithstanding the demonstrated superiority of alternatives. In the same way, the effects discussed above might be called "the politics of QWERTY."

An "Evolutionary" Perspective

If the distinction between policy rules and acts is one of degree rather than one of kind, and if rules are subject to erosion and reinterpretation while acts can create durable facts and institutions, then how should one view the policy process, and what are the appropriate roles for positive and normative analysis? In my judgment the required framework for analysis must be more flexible. It must be more dynamic, or even evolutionary, in the way it treats policy rules and acts. It should treat policymaking as a process that goes on in "real time," and constantly combines some features of rulemaking and some of individual acts, in varying degrees.

First, it is important to recognize that there are gradations among policy decisions even though there is no sharp binary dichotomy. Different policy decisions, whether concerning what one might label as a rule or as an act, have different degrees of permanence. For example, the general features of the tax system, such as the choice of income or value added as a base, and the principles used in defining the base, are as a whole quite durable, while the details like brackets and rates, or details of various exemptions, alter quite frequently. The principles underlying GATT, such as multilateralism and most favored nation, have on the whole proved more durable than the choices of whether and how to cover agriculture and services (at least they have served to stop even faster encroachment of nontariff barriers), and these in turn have proved more durable than the decisions of GATT panels on particular allegations of unfair trade.

An analogy with the Marshallian theory of industry equilibrium may prove helpful here. In that theory, some factors, typically labor, are supposed to be costlessly and quickly adjustable in the short run, while others, typically capital, are assumed inflexible once installed and can be reallocated only in the long run. The stylized dichotomy is useful when we want to introduce to beginning students the ideas of marginal costs, supply curves, and differing elasticities of supply in different timeframes. Beyond the level of introductory theory or in most practical applications, however, we know that factors differ in degree rather than in kind with regard to their costs of adjustment, and the real-time dynamics of a firm or an industry differs substantially from the simple picture of a passage from the Marshallian short run to the long run; see Dixit 1995 for a model of such dynamics. In the same manner, our view of the dynamics of the political process needs to advance from the simple dichotomy of constitutions versus policy acts to a richer version with gradations of permanence.

Second, as a corollary, one should admit that there are some degrees of freedom for policymaking at almost all times, more at some times than others. However, one must also recognize that the political process continues at all stages. There is no true veil of ignorance or unanimity on the infrequent occasions of major overhaul of the process; nor is the prospect for informing and persuading the participants totally excluded at the relatively minor points.

In other words, we should recognize that economic policymaking is a dynamic game, whose conditions are uncertain and changing, and whose rules are at least partially made by the participants as they go along. Each participant will try to manipulate the operation of the subsequent game to try to achieve an outcome that favors his or her own interests. The nature of these manipulations has been understood following the pioneering work of Schelling (1960): they are various commitments, some unconditional, others specifying response rules that are contingent on others' actions to come. Schelling calls such actions "strategic moves." Therefore, in this view of the policy process the degrees of freedom mostly consist of opportunities to make various strategic moves.

This evolutionary perspective can serve as a synthesis between the normative and the contractarian approaches to policy that were contrasted earlier. We can view each policy act, not as a choice to be made to maximize a social welfare function, but as an episode or play of the game within the set of existing rules and institutions, but admitting some leeway to make strategic moves that are capable of affecting or altering future rules and institutions. Conversely, we should view constitutions and rules, not as sacred texts written under ideal ex ante conditions of lack of conflict, leading to unanimity and providing a complete set of rules for the making of future policy acts, but as incomplete contracts that cope with a complex and changing world and contain some provisions for procedures to deal with unforeseen contingencies, yet are subject to explicit amendments as well as changes implicitly inflicted by policy acts.

1.4   A Theme: Transaction Costs

My review of the normative and positive alternatives in economic policy analysis has led me to a perspective that combines some of each, and yet differs from both in essential ways. I have argued that economic policymaking should be seen as an ongoing, imperfect, and incomplete process, with powerful but slow dynamics. This viewpoint has many similarities with the account of economic institutions that has been developed by Williamson, North, and others. The organizing concept for their analysis is that of *transaction costs*. These are to be interpreted very broadly, as the "comparative costs of planning, adapting, and monitoring task completion under alternative governance structures" (Williamson 1989, p. 142), or "the costs of measuring the valuable attributes of what is being exchanged and the costs of protecting rights and policing and enforcing agreements" (North 1990a, p. 27). In particular, the focus is on the evolution of governance

structures (institutions, contractual forms, etc.) to cope
with the transaction costs.

In the following chapters I will develop and illustrate
this idea into a conceptual framework for studying the political process of economic policymaking; following North
(1990b), I call it "transaction-cost politics." North examined
one particular manifestation of transaction costs, namely, a
lack of "instrumental rationality" of participants in the economic or political world: they use incorrect models of the
world to guide their actions, and the information feedback
they receive is not sufficient to cause them to revise the
models. I will examine a wider range of problems that are
attributable to transaction costs.

The idea of viewing the process of economic policy
through a transaction-cost lens is not new, any more than
ideas are ever new. Stephen Jay Gould expressed it bril-
liantly: "Pristine originality is an illusion" (1985, p. 335);
"ideas are 'in the air,' and several scholars simultaneously
wave their nets" (1980, pp. 47–48). There are numerous
previous articles that treat specific transaction costs that
arise in the making of economic policy, and some surveys
that make this connection more explicit. I will offer just a
few examples. The role of regulatory policies and agencies
in handling transaction costs has long been recognized
and analyzed by industrial organization theorists. The
importance of dynamics, incentive constraints, and politics
is recognized in the context of macroeconomic (monetary
and fiscal) policies; these constitute one kind of transaction
cost in Williamson's approach. Many models of macroeconomic policies have analyzed specific issues of this kind
(see Persson and Tabellini 1994a, Introduction, and the
articles collected there and in their 1994b). However, these
do not make any connection with Williamson's work.

Most of these macroeconomic models are theoretical, with only a little supporting evidence, but similar issues are recognized in practical discussions of policy, too. To give just one recent example, when Lindbeck et al. (1994) reexamined all aspects of Sweden's economic policy, they had a clear appreciation of the importance of politics, history and institutions (see especially pp. 13–21 and chapter 5).

However, I believe that my presentation of a complete transaction-cost perspective on economic policy analysis is a new contribution. I will examine a large variety of transaction costs that are encountered in the policy process, and some devices by which the system can ameliorate these costs. I will also look at some existing literature on positive political economy and attempt to place it within the transaction cost framework. This will give us a better understanding of each of these hitherto distinct lines of analysis, by showing us the scope of each in relation to that of the others. In the third chapter, I will look at two specific examples of policymaking where the transaction-cost approach helps improve our understanding of the operation of the processes and the institutions. The discussion of the general principles in the second chapter will also look ahead to, and draw on, these "case studies."

This framework of transaction-cost politics and the view of economic policymaking as a dynamic evolutionary process has considerable appeal, but it is open to some criticisms that I should attempt to defuse in advance.

First, I should clarify some self-imposed limitations. My focus is on the specific issue of the making of economic policy. Therefore I have taken for granted the larger issues and institutions of governance. Most important, I take for granted and do not discuss a prerequisite to all aspects of governance, namely, the existence of mechanisms of coercion, which is emphasized by Olson (1993). At a very basic level, a threat of force must underlie every political constitution. In an original position behind a veil of ignorance, everyone may voluntarily agree to a social contract, but the contract must include an explicit or implicit coercive mechanism to ensure continued participation after specific individual positions and interests have been revealed. All policy acts take place, and in particular, taxes are levied and collected, with this threat of force in the background. The power to coerce raises the possibility of its misuse. Although the intention of the constitution is that such force, or its threat, should serve the general interest, nothing can guarantee that once an agency is given the state's monopoly of force, it will not use this power in its own interest. Unless one interprets transaction costs in an excessively broad sense, their mere absence will not solve this problem because even though the initial social contract has specified the conditions of its operation in full detail, and even though every citizen can observe the misuse of power, the coercive force stops them from doing anything about it. Olson (1993) and McGuire and Olson (1995) show how in a repeated or ongoing governance relationship the coercive rulers' own interests can mitigate the problem and induce them to follow policies that are close to the general interest.

I have also excluded some narrower but more purely political issues from my analysis, for example, voting behavior and outcomes, legislative procedures and their manipulation, and so on, even though these often involve transaction-cost issues similar to the ones I consider. There are excellent surveys of research on these topics, for example, Mueller 1989 (especially chapters 4–12), Shepsle 1991 and Banks 1991, and at some point it may be worthwhile to connect them more explicitly with the family of transaction-cost analyses.

Theorists are likely to complain about the vagueness in the concept of transaction costs. These are defined so comprehensively that they cannot be put into a single unified and elegant model like the Arrow-Debreu or the Bergson-Samuelson models. Instead, we must construct dozens of separate small models, each of them treating only a part of the process, and then attempt to place each such model within an informal background understanding of the whole. In other words, transaction costs do not provide a single *analytical* framework, but only a loose *conceptual* framework for organizing many different analytical models. I respond by pointing out a parallel with the concept of oligopoly. There are so many different issues that arise in the study of competition among a small number of firms that there is no hope of constructing a single analytical model of oligopoly on par with the standard elegant model of perfect competition. However, most people would agree that oligopoly remains a useful conceptual umbrella for sheltering the large variety of models that examine specific issues such as tacit collusion, strategic commitments, and preemption. Similarly, I believe that transaction-cost politics provides a useful conceptual framework for organizing our thinking about economic policymaking. Of course, as Williamson (1985, p. xii) has stressed, the transaction-cost approach should be used in conjunction with, and not to the exclusion of, other approaches. My reason for emphasizing it here is that it has hitherto received less emphasis than it merits.

Practitioners are more likely to complain about some of the conclusions of the analysis. I will argue that the transactions-cost approach shows the need to accept some imperfection, and toleration of a slow process of coping using whatever instruments are at hand, economic and political; it does not offer any dramatic improvements or attainments of ideal outcomes that politicians like to claim and the public likes to hear. But this is the reality of policymaking, and we must learn to deal with it.

2   The Transaction-Cost Politics Framework

Why does the political process of economic policy matter? It obviously does, and some may be inclined to leave things at that and not delve into the reasons, but we can deepen our understanding of the issue by setting up an idealized hypothetical world where the political process would not matter. This is the world of the Coase theorem. If all participants in the economy could be brought together, if initial ownership rights to all economically valuable entities were assigned among these participants, and if they could costlessly make fully specified and fully binding agreements, then the outcome should be an efficient economic plan, leaving only the division of the spoils to be determined by the bargaining strengths of the participants.[1] There would be no role for politics.

Of course, the true value of the Coase theorem is not as a description of reality, but as an idealization or benchmark

---

1. For detailed discussions, see Demsetz 1964 and Buchanan 1973. Remember that I am taking for granted the existence of a governance structure that assigns initial rights and enforces voluntary agreements to trade these rights; see Olson 1993 for issues raised by this. There remain problems, for example the core may be empty for certain allocations of property rights in some situations of external diseconomies (Shapley and Shubik 1969), but these are not central to my present purpose.

that serves to focus our attention on the specific ways in which the reality differs from the ideal, and the consequences of these departures. The real task is to recognize, categorize, and study the multitude of these causes and their effects.

In economic relationships—contracts, firms, and markets—the reasons for failure of the Coase theorem have been termed "transaction costs," using the term in a very broad and generalized sense: anything that impedes the specification, monitoring, or enforcement of an economic transaction is a transaction cost. The work of Williamson and others over the last two decades has given us a good understanding of the nature and the effects of these costs, and Williamson (1989) has given a good summary of the taxonomy and analysis of transaction costs in the context of industrial organization. All forms of these costs exist, in many cases with greater strength, in political processes. By analogy with Williamson's name "transaction-cost economics" for the study of the effects of transaction costs on economic organizations and outcomes, such a framework might be called "transaction-cost politics." In this chapter I elaborate on this theme of transaction-cost politics and its implications for economic policy. A natural way to begin is by examining the ways in which the political process fails to produce the ideal outcome of the Coase benchmark. That will pave the way for the analysis of the reasons for this failure.

2.1 Political Outcomes and Economic Efficiency

If the conditions of the Coase theorem are met, the outcome has strong properties of economic efficiency. No transaction that can benefit some group of people without hurting others goes unconsummated; no Pareto improvement goes unrealized. Departures from the benchmark correspondingly create a presumption of inefficiency. There does seem to be a presumption that the political process operates particularly inefficiently in its attempts to influence economic outcomes. Krugman (1990, p. xi) characterized recent times as "the age of diminished expectations, an era in which our economy has not delivered very much but in which there is little political demand that it do better." He was speaking of the United States' economy, but in the last few years similar thoughts have been expressed with regard to Europe and Japan. Krugman merely lists various symptoms of economic malaise, and offers little mention and no analysis of the nature and causes of the political failures that have dampened people's expectations from governments.

However, the transaction technology and the limitations it imposes on economic possibilities are just as real as the production technology and its limitations. Stiglitz has repeatedly emphasized this with regard to information asymmetries, and Williamson's analysis of other kinds of transaction costs reinforces the point. Therefore our test of whether an outcome is inefficient needs to recognize the constraints imposed by transaction costs just as much as we respect resource and technology constraints. Williamson (1996, p. 195) calls this the test of *remediableness*. He defines this idea as saying that "an outcome for which no feasible superior alternative can be described and implemented with net gains is presumed to be efficient." The words "feasible" and "implemented" must be understood properly—the reference is mainly to the transactions technology of the political or administrative process. Williamson and others have also pointed out that in all interactions subject to transaction costs, it is in the interests of the participants to devise methods, market or nonmarket, official or private, by which such costs can be mitigated, and that the success of such devices will depend on related institutions, the history and the likely future duration of the interaction, and so on. Many seemingly inefficient practices of firms, and their market or contract outcomes, are revealed on closer scrutiny to be quite creditable attempts to cope with difficult transaction cost problems. Therefore one should not jump from the observation of an apparent inefficiency to the assertion of a remedy; one should examine the organization of firms and the institutions of transactions more closely to look for any mechanisms to cope with transaction costs, and ask how well they do their job. When we judge a mechanism whose function is to cope with a complex and changing world, flexibility and adaptability have value. I will argue that we can see such coping mechanisms in many political organizations and outcomes. However, an example of the general presumption of the inefficacy of politics will provide a useful starting point for the study of transaction costs in politics.

Consider the form of policies to help declining industries, agriculture, and so on. These are often protected from import competition using trade barriers, increasingly quotas or "voluntary" restraint agreements, which in nearly every instance impose very large costs on the domestic users of these products. The balance of benefits to the stakeholders in the industry and the costs to the rest of the country is negative, and often quite substantial. Any economist would suggest far better policies. At the top of this list will be direct lump sum grants that compensate the stakeholders for their losses and then leave them free to seek and find the best alternative uses for their resources. Next would be retraining and relocation grants to assist the movement of resources to the better uses. Instead of any of these policies, we observe policies like tariff and quota protection, price supports, or subsidies, which actually encourage the resources to remain in their declining and less productive uses while inflicting higher prices on users of the products or higher burdens on the taxpayers.

The economists' standard explanation of the prevalence of such inefficient policies rests on a particular model of the operation of special-interest politics. The benefits of the inefficient policies accrue as large per capita amounts to a small and concentrated special-interest group, while their costs fall in small per capita amounts on a large and diffuse population. The former has a substantial incentive to become informed about their benefits and solve the free-rider problem involved in taking political action, whereas the latter have a much smaller incentive and therefore remain uninformed and unorganized. For example, Marks (1993) has estimated that in the late 1980s, the United States sugar price supports and import restrictions cost consumers about $11.50 per head, while each of about ten thousand sugar-beet farms benefitted by $50,000, and each of a thousand sugarcane farms by as much as $500,000. So consumers stay silent, whereas producers' voices are loud and government agencies respond to them.

This theory goes back at least as far as Olson (1965); Wilson (1989, chapter 5) has given a well-known recent account and labeled it "client politics." This explanation has some force and must be a part of the answer, but it is not complete and leaves room for other forces and theories.

First, despite appearances, the sugar industry does not provide a very good example of client politics. Over 70 percent of purchases of sugar in the United States are by industrial users—soft drink manufacturers, bakers and confectioners and so on—who benefit from lower sugar prices and can form pressure groups to resist price-raising protectionist policies just as easily as sugar-growing interests can lobby for protection. In fact these users' groups have been passive or even supportive of the growers' interests; this remains a puzzle (Krueger 1990). Even without such potential countervailing lobbyists, the political process should produce forces that promote efficient policies. It is true that no individual consumer in the United States has much to gain by acquiring information and taking action to reduce the price of sugar. But a candidate looking for an attractive issue stands to gain a great deal by informing these consumers as a whole and proposing better policies that will attract their votes. In other words, a "political entrepreneur" can expend the resources needed to acquire information and take action, and attempt to exploit the "political arbitrage" that is inherent in the initial inefficient situation.

Of course we should not expect such arbitrage to work perfectly: people start out with some skepticism about politicians' assertions; there is room for hired guns of special interests to produce competing figures in attempts to disinform the voters; and incumbents have every incentive and sufficiently deep pockets to engage in predatory entry deterrence against such arbitragers. North (1990b, pp. 360–361) emphasizes several of these aspects; but Arnold (1990) argues that the political payoff to politicians from publicizing hidden but potentially large economic cost, and from creating issue positions that solve the free-rider problem for the bearers of these costs, is real and often effective. He argues that the prospect of such political entrepreneurship does constrain the ability of members of the United States Congress to legislate special favors for even the highly organized and informed minorities. Wilson (1989, pp. 83–86) also argues that improvements in the technology of political organization and the lowering of institutional barriers to access have reduced the extent of client politics in the United States in recent years. Therefore it is necessary to improve and deepen the standard political theory of inefficient outcomes. Some recent work (Dixit and Londregan 1995, 1996), offers such an explanation based on the idea of credibility. The workers in an industry that experiences a negative shock because of technological shifts or the growth of import competition face the prospect of lower incomes over the next several years or even decades. An economically efficient solution would be to compensate them for the capitalized value of these losses in a lump sum, and then leave them to find and take up their best alternative opportunities. The political process is not going to offer such capital sums up front, because the recipients cannot credibly promise their votes over the next several elections that span the duration of their prospective income loss. Therefore any compensation will have to take the form of a gradual stream of payments lasting several years. Then the question of credibility switches to the other side. Political candidates and parties can renege on their promises to the workers if that becomes politically advantageous in the future. The workers know that their receipt of compensation in the future will depend on their future political power, not on the economic choices they make to stay in the declining industry or move to a new industry or location. In fact they may suspect that moving will disperse their forces and reduce their political strength. Therefore their incentives to relocate to more productive opportunities are blunted, and they use their political power to demand and get help in their current occupation. If the political process could make an initial binding contract that would promise compensation streams to the workers conditional on their moving away from the declining industry, an outcome could be designed to be better for everyone. But such long-term contracts are not feasible; any promises to reward efficient economic relocation choices, or equally, any threats to withhold benefits to those who fail to make such choices, are not credible.[2]

The problem of credibility, or more generally of the time consistency of policy, is another kind of transaction cost in Williamson's terminology, and the purpose of the example is to make that very point. Even if we regard the "concentrated benefits, diffuse costs" model as an inadequate explanation of the success of protectionist policies, other explanations we prefer are also likely to come from the same general family of transaction costs.

There are several other sources of such costs, and they all introduce departures from the Coasean benchmark of efficient outcomes that maximize total economic benefits and then negotiate to divide them up. We can pose the question of efficiency or remediability of policies and compare alternative hypotheses and theories within this overarching framework of transaction costs. We should recognize the whole broad categories of these costs, or the whole class of frictions that pervade the political process. Finally, as in economics, we must recognize that the participants in the process have natural, endogenous incentives to reduce such transaction costs or to minimize their effects, and we must examine various mechanisms by which political processes and institutions will attempt to do so. I have proposed

2. A recent more general discussion of efficiency and inefficiency in political equilibria is in Besley and Coate 1994, 1995; the latter has a related dynamic model based on infeasibility of commitment.

labeling this framework "transaction-cost politics." In the rest of this section, I will develop this theme in somewhat greater detail.

2.2 Transaction-Cost Analysis in Politics

The pioneering work of Coase, Williamson, North, and others has led to the recognition that various transaction costs are the primary reason why impersonal competitive markets do not function as effectively as might be suggested by the neoclassical benchmark of the Arrow-Debreu theory or the corresponding more general benchmark of the Aumann-Shapley core in cooperative game theory, which forms the theoretical underpinning of the Coase theorem. That in turn explains the emergence of different mechanisms and institutions as devices that enable the participants to mitigate or to cope with the transaction costs. This mode of analysis has been developed and tested most fully in industrial economics and in economic history (see, respectively, Williamson 1989 and North 1990a).

The idea of studying the political process in the transaction-cost mode originates with North (1990b).[3] His main focus is on a particular facet of transaction costs, namely, a failure of "instrumental rationality" for participants in the process. The informational feedback is inadequate to convey to these participants the correct theory of how their world operates; this affects the individuals' decisions and in turn the outcome of the process and the information it generates. However, there are other aspects of transaction costs that are also prominent in industrial economics. They are to do with game-theoretic issues of asymmetric

---

3. Wilson (1989, p. 358) briefly mentions it as an idea that is unexplored but worth attention.

information and time-consistency of action, and they persist and affect outcomes even if there is full instrumental rationality, that is, even when every participant knows the correct theory of the world and can perfectly calculate his own optimal strategy. The problems arise in the strategic interaction between such individuals and the equilibrium of their game. Therefore the scope of transaction-cost analysis is much broader than that examined by North.

Much recent formal modeling in political economy is close to this tradition of industrial economics in emphasizing transaction costs, but the connection does not appear to have been explicitly recognized or exploited. Two classes of examples will make the point. First, numerous analyses of time-consistency and commitment in fiscal and monetary policy derive from Kydland and Prescott's (1977) work on rules versus discretion. Difficulties with credibility of commitments constitute an important class of transaction costs. Second, problems of agency in politics and administration have been studied by several researchers (see the surveys in Banks 1991 and Persson and Tabellini 1990, expositions of related ideas and models in Tirole 1994 and Laffont 1995, and recent research like Grossman and Helpman 1994). Agency problems involving moral hazard and opportunism, and the costs of mitigating or controlling these informational asymmetries, are some of the major transaction costs that Williamson and others have emphasized in industrial economics.

North's (1990b) analysis of transaction-cost politics leads him to the conclusion that we should expect political markets to be even more beset by transaction costs, and therefore operate even less efficiently, than economic markets. His emphasis is on the effect of information costs on individual decisionmaking (what he calls a lack of instrumental rationality). Here I develop a broader theme, involving a larger class of problems that have been studied in transaction-cost economics (TCE), and examine how a corresponding problem in transaction-cost politics (TCP) will be similar or different. My classification mostly derives from Williamson 1989.

This review of how various transaction costs affect the political process reinforces the conclusion that North reached in his setting—in almost all other dimensions of transaction costs, too, political processes seem likely to be even more beset by transaction costs than are economic relationships. Of course the analysis cannot rest there. We should expect to see some systemic attempts to cope with the transaction costs and to mitigate their ill-effects. This occurs through the process of institutional and organizational change, which is itself history-dependent and often quite slow; see North (1990b) for this theme. Therefore the extent of the problems posed by transaction costs, and the extent to which they can be solved, will vary with the specific context of the country, the bloc, or the international body involved. I will examine various mechanisms to cope with transaction costs, and their applications, after the taxonomy of the costs has been developed.

FTAs as a "response" to failure of multi-lateralism

2.2.1 Background of Transaction-Cost Analysis

As a preliminary to the taxonomy of transaction costs, we should be clear about some background conditions or assumptions of the transaction-cost framework. I proceed by briefly describing what transaction-cost economics (TCE) has to say about each point and then develop the corresponding idea for transaction-cost politics (TCP).

The Contract as Unit of Analysis

In TCE, the basic unit of analysis is a "contract" or a single transaction between two parties in an economic relationship. The contracts are generally promises whereby one party agrees to take an action of economic value to the other, in return for some reciprocal action or a payment. These actions are generally taken with different degrees of observability, at different points in time, and with different degrees of sunkenness or reversibility. The relationship itself can have different degrees of continuity. For these reasons, the parties to the contract have varying degrees of natural voluntary incentives to fulfill the terms of their mutual promises. In TCE, an external contract-enforcement agency, namely the legal institution governing the contract, is assumed to exist, although its performance is again constrained by the difficulties of verifying whether, or how well or badly, the parties have met the conditions of the contract, and it is recognized that sometimes bilateral private mechanisms of dispute resolution may outperform external enforcement. In other words, TCE assumes that contracts are enforceable within the limits of the existing legal institutions and the available information.

In TCP, the parties to a political contract are citizens (individuals or interest-group organizations), on the one hand, and politicians (individuals or parties) or administrators (regulatory agencies, etc.), on the other. The contract is a promise of a policy (or program) in return for votes (or contributions). Once we go beyond this basic parallel, however, political contracts differ from economic contracts in several ways, all of which make them more complex and harder to enforce.

First, political contracts are rarely between two clearly identifiable contractors; they have multiple parties (voters or lobbyists) on at least one side of the relationship. Second, their terms are generally much more vague than those of economic contracts. They leave much room for interpretation, and many loopholes for escape and opportunities to blame third parties or force majeure for failure to deliver. Thus a promise to cut taxes rarely specifies by how much, and can be rescinded when the budget situation turns out to be much worse than expected.[4]

Contract Enforcement

At a very basic level, a threat of force underlies every political constitution. In an original position behind a veil of ignorance, everyone may voluntarily agree on a social contract, but the contract must include an explicit or implicit coercive mechanism to ensure continued participation after specific individual positions have been revealed. All policy acts take place, and in particular, taxes are levied and collected, with this threat of force in the background. Olson (1993) puts such mechanisms with coercive capability at the center of his theory of the emergence and performance of governments. The power to coerce raises the danger of its misuse. Although the intention of the constitution is that such force, or its threat, should serve the general interest, nothing can guarantee that once an agency is given the state's monopoly of force, it will not use this power in pursuit of its own interests. Ultimately, the answer to the question: "Who guards the guardians?" must be: "No one." But it may be possible to structure the rulers' incentives in

---

4. There are rare exceptions like George Bush's pledge in the 1988 presidential election, "Read my lips, no new taxes." This became a commitment, and the fact that Bush retreated from it in 1990, albeit as a part of negotiations with the Congress, came back to haunt him in the 1992 election.

such a way that they will find it in their own interests to
remain reasonably benevolent. McGuire and Olson (1995)
have examined the performance of alternative governance
arrangements from this point of view and have shown that
rulers who have a sufficiently large and stable interest in
the economy act in ways that are remarkably consistent
with the interests of the governed.

However, many political promises are not subject to any
external enforcement mechanism. The courts do not perform this role. In the United States, increasingly in the European Union, and in some other countries, the judiciary is
an effective guardian of the constitution and may bar the
government from taking certain actions even if they were
promised, but the judiciary cannot compel actions to fulfill
campaign promises. If a politician fails to deliver on such a
"contractual obligation," the only recourse to the other side
is to remove him or her from office. In a democracy that
means defeating them in an election, which can be difficult
because elections involve multiple issues in which a single
breach of promise may not be the determining one. Removing nondemocratic governments from office is even harder.
In most cases there is little or no outside enforcement, and
there can be no monetary penalties or compensation for
broken promises.

In fact there is one economic relationship that is more
closely parallel to the political contract, namely, the "contract" between the shareholders of a firm and its managers
or the board of directors. The management's promise to
the owners of equity is specified only in the vaguest terms,
namely, general fiduciary responsibility. This is hard to verify, particularly since the management controls much of the
relevant information. The shareholders also face the problems of organizing to outvote the management. This anal-

ogy between political contracts and equity contracts may be worth further exploration.

Governance Structures
TCE views firms as governance structures, replacing the neoclassical view of them as production functions. In the latter, once the quantities of inputs used in a production process are specified, exogenous technological considerations will fix the quantity of output (or an efficient frontier linking quantities of multiple outputs). In the TCE view, the differing degrees of sunkenness of different inputs will affect the behavior of their owners, unobservability of quality or effort will influence the effectiveness of other inputs, managerial quality and effort will determine how well the inputs are combined, and so on. The mechanisms that are in place to counter these transaction-cost problems, for example, incentive schemes, will also influence the behavior of the various parties. In other words, organizational and governance structures of firms will have an important impact on what they do. Since the neoclassical view dominated economic theory for many years, the insights of TCE were at first novel and revolutionary.

Political institutions and organizations *are* governance structures and are well recognized as such, so in this respect TCP is ahead of TCE.

Governance structures are characterized by various agency relationships. In a firm, for example, the managers act as agents of the equity owners, who are the principals. The hierarchy of a firm often involves other agency relations, for example between managers and line supervisors, or purchasers and outside suppliers. The general idea is that the interests of the parties to a transaction are at least partially in conflict, and the agent has some information or action advantage over the principal. The standard model of operation of an agency is one where the principal devises a scheme of incentives or penalties, such that the agent's action is altered at least partially in the direction that favors the principal's interest. This typically requires a trade-off between efficiency and risksharing, and the result is a second-best.

Agency relationships are often more complex in the political than in the economic context. Most important, it is not always clear who is whose agent. Different models have taken different views on this. In many models of political signaling, reviewed by Banks (1991) and Persson and Tabellini (1990), one finds the citizens or voters as principals and the candidates or parties as agents. (In Soviet-type economies, the Communist Party was the principal and the citizens were the agents, a few of them double agents.) In others, we find the whole legislature as the principal and a specialist committee as the agent, or a leader or hegemon as the principal and the followers as agents. In many models of macroeconomic politics, the government or the treasury is the principal and the central bank the agent.

The question of agency may seem clear for a bureaucracy: agencies are created as parts of the legislative or the executive branches of government and are formally responsible to the Congress or the president respectively; but in reality the lines of authority are blurred. Each branch wields some power over the other's agents, and others have some influence, for example, courts, interest groups, and the media. The fact that each government agency or bureaucracy is simultaneously answerable to multiple principals, who are trying to influence its actions in different directions, is emphasized by Wilson (1989), and I will examine it in greater detail below.

Bounded Rationality

Orthodox economic analysis assumes that all individuals know the true model of the world and costlessly calculate their optimal actions, although the more recent versions recognize various informational limitations under which they do this calculation. TCE recognizes that the possible states of the world are very complex, and individuals' knowledge of the workings of the world is very imperfect. This affects the actions of individuals as well as the transactions among them. Most importantly, individuals cannot condition these transactions on extremely complex and even unknown future contingencies. In other words, all feasible contracts are necessarily incomplete. Therefore, ex post institutions (dispute-settlement mechanisms) are very important. But the very complexity of nature makes these mechanisms less than perfect—the state of the world may not be observable ex post, or even if observed by the parties to the contract, may not be verifiable to an outsider whose job is to enforce it.

In TCP such complexity and uncertainty is even more pronounced. Explicit contracts that make political promises contingent upon various international developments, domestic shifts of opinion, and so forth, would be impossibly complex. In many instances explicit contracts of this kind between economic interests and politicians or bureaucrats are tantamount to bribery and therefore simply illegal, and imperfect clandestine or informal substitutes for them emerge. Dispute-settlement mechanisms are even less effective because they must be internal to the process (e.g., election or impeachment). For all these reasons, political contracts are even less complete than economic ones, and bounded rationality has more serious bite.

The extent of the difficulty varies across countries and times. When a country has been governed by a close-knit group of politicians and civil servants working in collaboration with business and labor groups, they can reduce some of the uncertainty because of the mutual trust of their ongoing relationships. Some European countries over the past century, or Japan for the four decades from the 1950s to the 1980s, may be cases in point. But such closed governance systems are becoming less prevalent and less successful. Japan has undergone some fundamental changes; the European Union is likely to be too heterogeneous and too much influenced by its sovereign members. In the context of international relations, the General Agreement on Tariffs and Trade (GATT) was an example of a process that was rendered ineffective because of the uncertainty generated by its weak dispute resolution mechanisms.

2.2.2   A Taxonomy of Transaction Costs

With the above background, we can now examine some important forms of transaction costs and begin to describe their effects on the operation of the policy process. Once again, I proceed by comparing transaction-cost economics (TCE) and politics (TCP).

Information-Impactedness
The term "information-impactedness" was introduced by Williamson to capture all aspects of limited and asymmetric information. It has a close parallel in the work of Stiglitz and others in information economics, where the corresponding concept is split into three different aspects: (1) a precontract informational advantage for one of the parties (adverse selection, leading to signaling

and screening costs); (2) nonobservability of the agent's action (moral hazard, leading to costs of monitoring or incentive schemes); and (3) nonverifiability of information to outsiders (leading to auditing costs or the costs due to misrepresentation when an audit is too costly).

In TCP, if there are no outside dispute-settlement mechanisms anyway, then nothing further is lost by the lack of verifiability. It still inflicts costs on the transaction because parties will take actions in anticipation of this lack of verification; for example, they will underinvest. Other kinds of information asymmetries, namely, adverse selection and moral hazard, are often more prevalent and more serious in TCP; for example, political parties' true intentions are often hidden behind their publicly announced platforms. The voters must then try to infer the truth from observations of actions. In information economics, this is the problem of signaling and screening; and it can lead to one of two types of outcomes, separation (where actions accurately reveal the truth) or pooling (where agents with two or more underlying characteristics take the same action and therefore cannot be distinguished). In either case there can be costs; in the separation case the agents with good qualities must take some costly action to distinguish themselves credibly from others who resemble them but have poorer qualities, whereas in the pooling case the poorer types take costly actions to get themselves confused with the better types, and there is loss of information. The client politics models belong to this category, as do many of the models surveyed in Banks 1990.

Opportunism
In TCE, when actions of agents are unobservable, they are subject to moral hazard. The need to control it implies the

need for suitable ex ante mechanisms (monitoring schemes and incentive-payment contracts) as well as ex post ones (auditing and penalties, or similar other safeguards). Agency relationships in TCP are much more complicated. There are frequent occurrences of multiple agency, both horizontal (cabinet government, decentralized jurisdictions) and vertical (electorate, politician and civil servant; federal, state, and local; etc.). Similarly, there is frequent common agency (politicians beholden to, or bureaucrats answerable to, multiple interest groups). Monitoring of some branches (legislative and judiciary) is constant in the media, but that of others (executive, especially many of its departments and agencies) is much harder. Wilson (1989) has emphasized this multiplicity and complexity of agency relationships in politics and public administration. Also, as was pointed out above in another context, the incentives and safeguards must be largely internal to the political process.

The net result is that the political process cannot use monitoring and incentive contracts to the same extent that they are used in economic relationships. Instead, we see much greater reliance on more blunt instruments — commitments and constraints. These issues are discussed in more detail below.

Asset Specificity
Opportunism arises in a particular way, combining dynamic inconsistency with moral hazard, when in a contract between two parties to exploit a mutually profitable opportunity, at least one party must generally make an irreversible investment. Once it has done so, it will become vulnerable to demands of the other party to renegotiate the contract and get for itself a greater share of profit, made

under the threat of dissolving the whole relationship. This makes even ex ante competitive relationships ex post bilateral. If unresolved, this problem would lead to severe underinvestment because the party contemplating its investment decision would look ahead and recognize that its return on the investment is going to be expropriated by the other. In turn, both parties recognize that they both stand to lose by letting this problem remain unresolved; therefore they attempt to reduce the risk of such expropriation. This can be accomplished using various ex ante provisions. It may be possible to arrange a balancing specific investment by the other party that places the two at each other's mercy and therefore behaving well. Or the investor may be given a "hostage" belonging to the other, so that any expropriative demand by the other would be met by seizure of the hostage. There may also be ex post safeguards, for example, fines or compensation.

There are similar aspects of dynamic inconsistency within the political process itself, but more important, these also interact with the performance of the economy. Thus economic investments in specific assets may be deterred by fear of political hold-up (policy switch); politicians with specific assets (in locations, industries, etc.) and their pivotal supporters with economic specific investments (human or physical capital specific to an industry) may together conspire to cause a lock-in of policy. Dixit and Londregan (1995) develop a model where the anticipation of future political success keeps workers inefficiently in declining industries.

Moe (1990) makes a related point. The favors given to an interest group by one political party may be overturned if the other party or even a new faction comes to power. This uncertainty concerning "political property rights" leads the groups to make political compromises and develop economically inefficient mechanisms that are less prone to such reversals. Laffont and Tirole (1993, chapter 16) and Tirole (1994, p. 17) have an argument that goes further. At any one time, the government is controlled by one political party or another, favoring one special interest or another. If the government of the day were allowed to lock in the policy by a long-term commitment that exceeds its own expected life, this may preclude changes that would be demanded by future majorities. Thus constitutional provisions that preclude such commitments may serve a useful purpose.

But these arguments are open to two objections. First, it is not evident that a shift in political power always leads to a reversal of interest groups' fortunes. Indeed, many groups that are pivotal in the political spectrum are courted by both parties (see Lindbeck and Weibull 1987 and Dixit and Londregan 1996). Also, a process of logrolling can form a grand coalition that guarantees benefits to all the organized interest groups (see Shepsle and Weingast 1981). Second, it is not clear why inefficient mechanisms should necessarily be harder to reverse than efficient ones.

2.2.3   Themes of Transaction-Cost Analysis

Next comes a brief look at some general methodological principles that operate in transaction-cost analysis and how they differ between TCE and TCP.

Comparative Institutional Analysis
TCE builds upon the idea that institutions and organizations seek to achieve efficiency, minimizing a comprehensive cost—inclusive not merely of the neoclassical production cost, but also of transaction costs of the kind

discussed. Sometimes the task is made easier by the fact that competitive product markets contain a natural-selection-like external force that is conducive to the evolution of such efficiency; firms with the best organization will do best, attract more capital, and grow, while those with poor organization will have high costs, and will decline and die in the market. In reality the selection mechanism also works very imperfectly; in the uncertain and nonstationary environment of the real world, a firm with its given organizational structure may do well and then suddenly meet new conditions to which it is poorly placed to adapt. But the existence of the selection mechanism provides some discipline and some limit to the waste that can exist in an organization.

In TCP, the forces of selection and evolution — elections, changes in party membership and platforms, and so forth — are weaker and slower, so the presumption of efficiency must also be weaker. In fact political authorities can sometimes manipulate information and hide from the citizens the facts about their lack of success. Thus they can slow down the forces of selection and evolution; observe how the regimes in former communist countries of eastern Europe succeeded for decades by controlling their citizens' information and thinking, but how they suddenly became untenable soon after their citizenry achieved widespread access to Western news media like satellite broadcasting.

The political process does have several ways of ameliorating transaction costs, and I will examine some in the next subsection.

Performance Criteria
The analysis of TCE forces us to conclude that efficiency of an economic institution should be judged on a systemic

basis, considering ex ante and ex post arrangements together, and not on its performance in any particular state
of the world.

Political systems should also be judged on such a basis.
To give a trivial example, the U.S. Department of Defense
is often criticized because, inclusive of administrative cost,
it pays absurdly large sums to procure small items, like
the notorious $435 hammer. The criticism fails to recognize
that an alternative system that delegates such purchase decisions to lower-level managers may be misused by them
and lead to its own waste.[5] (Of course a better solution may
be to delegate the authority but restrict the manager's total
budget for small procurements.)

There is an added dimension. Substantial economies
of scope exist across different problems of economic and
social policy. Therefore political organizations are multi-
purpose entities: the same local government looks after
education, trash pick-up, and policing, even though the
optimal arrangement for each problem considered in isolation may be different. Such bodies may not be efficient
always and in every use (even considering ex ante and ex
post in that use jointly). We should only look for efficiency
in an average sense over their functions. Just as TCE asks
us to look at efficiency in an average sense over time,
TCP should tell us to look for efficiency averaged over
time and function together. Actually, the duration of the
system and its future functions cannot be specified fully
in advance. Therefore, when we judge such a system, we
should recognize the value of adaptability.

---

5. See Wilson's (1989, pp. 319–20) discussion of military procurement for
the truth behind such episodes and some justification of the procurement
systems.

Wilson (1989, chapter 17) makes a further point. When several principals control a common agency, the concept of efficiency must recognize the divergent interests of these principals. The process and its outcomes may look inefficient from an economist's viewpoint, but they may be the best feasible ways of serving other legitimate interests such as accountability and horizontal equity. I will examine this issue of common agency in more detail below.

2.3 Mechanisms to Cope with Transaction Costs in Politics

Transaction-cost economics recognizes that all parties to an economic transaction can benefit if they can develop ways to economize on transaction costs, just as they can reap mutual gains by economizing on resource costs of production, for example, by specializing according to comparative advantage. Of course, each of the participants has some divergence of interests from that of the others, some informational advantage, and some freedom of action. Therefore, the institutions or processes must evolve to ameliorate the problems like opportunism, either with feasible external enforcement mechanisms or with credible internal ones. Indeed, the success or failure of economic ventures and transactions can depend on the ability of the participants to devise such institutions and enforcement mechanisms (see Greif 1993 for historical analyses bearing on this).

The same idea applies in principle to political interactions. There is clear potential benefit from economizing on transaction costs. Rules and institutions should, and do, evolve to serve this purpose. The precise nature of the institution depends on the nature of the problem to be addressed. Also, as we saw above, transaction costs are more pervasive in politics, and external enforcement mechanisms are less available or less effective. Therefore, we should expect to see some differences between economic and political systems in the way they cope with transaction costs. In this section I will develop this theme, by focusing on different kinds of political transaction costs and examining some examples of coping mechanisms that we can think of or observe.

2.3.1 Commitment

Since opportunism arises from the freedom of ex post action, an obvious way to control it is to make a precommitment that limits this freedom. The device of commitment is probably the one most discussed in theoretical analyses of transaction-cost politics, as well as the one most attempted in practice. Of course, a commitment must be credible if it is to have the desired effect. To be credible, in turn, the commitment must be (1) clear and observable to all ex ante, and (2) irreversible ex post. In practice, credibility is not an all-or-nothing matter, just as the dichotomy between constitutions and acts is not a clear binary choice. There are degrees of credibility, and the success of each commitment device depends on the degree it can achieve.

Commitments carry a cost, namely, the sacrifice of flexibility. In principle one could make a commitment to a contingent rule, which will specify the precise actions to be taken in all future eventualities, but this is often too complex to be feasible. Further, not all conceivable eventualities may be foreseen, and one may wish to leave some generalized freedom to respond to a genuinely new or unforeseen circumstance. Of course, such "force majeure" provisions constitute loopholes that can be used to escape from commitments and therefore undermine the credibility that one seeks. This trade-off is resolved differently in different contexts, and the outcomes vary correspondingly.

Theoretical analysis of problems of time-consistency and commitment began in the arena of macroeconomic policy with the famous 1977 article of Kydland and Prescott. They pointed out that in a dynamic economy, the policymaker often has ex post incentives to renege on a policy that may have been optimal ex ante. There are two famous examples of this. First, over the long haul, low or zero inflation may be optimal, but at any time there can be short-term gains from surprise inflation, either in the form of a higher level of employment or larger seignorage revenues to the government. If the policymaker is free to give way to such an ex post temptation, however, the public will recognize this and alter its own behavior (labor supply or money holding) in such a way that the outcome is worse than that where the ex ante optimal policy is always adhered to. Second, the economy's supply of capital is fixed in the short run, but very elastic in the long run. Since the theory of optimal taxation tells us that the deadweight burden per unit of revenue at the margin is inversely related to the elasticity of response, the ex ante policy that is an optimal plan over the long haul is one of very low or even zero taxation of capital (see Lucas 1990 for a recent statement of this), but in any short run the policymaker has the temptation to generate extra revenue without creating any distortion by taxing the returns to the inelastically supplied stock of capital at that instant. Of course, if people recognize this, they will not invest, and the economy's dynamic path will be suboptimal.

This problem can arise even if the policymaker is the benevolent dictator of the normative approach to policy design, whose objective is the maximization of social welfare, so long as this dictator retains the freedom to choose a new policy action at every instant. In fact it is exactly the temptation to use future instruments to secure an even greater improvement in social welfare that, when anticipated by the private sector, leads "paradoxically" to a worse outcome.

In such cases, everyone stands to gain if the policymaker can forgo the discretion and credibly commit to a policy rule. A possible minor confusion should be clarified. A rule can specify the future path of policy unconditionally, for example, a constant or a sure time-path for the rate of inflation or the capital tax rate, or it could be a conditional-response rule, which states the actual policy that will be adopted as a function of other variables, including external uncertainty and the private sector's response. The latter kind of rule is guaranteed to be better than discretion. It is always *feasible* to choose a rule specifying exactly those responses that would occur in a policy regime allowing full discretion, so the *optimal* contingent-response rule cannot do worse. However, an unconditional rule is not guaranteed to do better than discretion.

We must therefore look for mechanisms and institutions that can allow the government to make credible commitments to policy rules. The general theory of credibility goes back to Schelling (1960), and has been substantially enriched and developed in formal game-theoretic models (see also Dixit and Nalebuff 1991, chapter 6 for a classification and illustrations of commitment devices). The theoretical literature on credibility in macroeconomic policy has examined several possible devices of this kind; here are some of the best-studied.

Locking-in Actions

Schelling (1960, p. 24) expresses, with his characteristic clarity and simplicity, the answer to the question of how one can persuade another person to believe that one is going to act in a certain way in the future: "Make it true." One can take an action in advance, for example, alter one's preferences demonstrably, or restrict one's own future freedom of action, so that the choice one wants to commit to becomes optimal, or even the only one available.

In the theory of macro policy, the simplest example of this device is to structure the government's debt so as to maintain a zero net nominal balance of credit or debt with the private sector. This eliminates the ex post temptation to create surprise inflation (see Persson, Persson, and Svensson 1987). Many of the devices that are discussed later also achieve their credibility with the aid of some locking-in action taken in advance.

Delegation

An action that removes one's future freedom of action is to give the power to take that action to someone else who does not suffer from the same temptation of opportunism, because this delegate has either different preferences or a simple mandate to act in a particular way.

In the analysis of macroeconomic policy, the standard example of this principle is the benefit from delegating monetary policy to a central bank, which is more "conservative" than the government in the sense that it places more weight on the costs of inflation (see Rogoff 1985 and the discussion in Persson and Tabellini 1994a, Introduction). Commitment to a fixed exchange rate has some similar aspects.

These examples also demonstrate a trade-off between the competing benefits of commitment and flexibility. Commitment has value because if the government were free to respond to its ex post opportunities in every future contingency, the private sector's response in anticipation of such behavior would lead to a worse outcome for the economy over time. However, if the government is not free to respond to adverse future conditions flexibly, that can create its own cost in terms of future economic performance. This cost was demonstrated vividly in the context of the European exchange-rate mechanism in 1992. Many countries pegged their exchange rate to the German mark, thereby committing their governments to pursue a monetary policy that was no more inflationary than that of the famously conservative Bundesbank. Then, when these countries needed a real devaluation relative to the mark because of growing productivity differentials or some such reasons, they were unable to achieve it with the simpler device of changing the nominal exchange rate and had to use deflationary domestic policies that inflicted a large cost in the form of unemployment and lost output. Ultimately, they were forced to abandon their exchange-rate targets, thereby losing the credibility as well.

This conflict between commitment and flexibility could be handled in principle by committing the government, not to an unconditional rule, but to a rule that specifies exactly which contingencies it can respond to and how. In practice such rules become too complex to be usable. Sometimes the flexibility they provide can be manipulated by a future government, thereby eliminating their commitment value. For both these reasons, practical rules have to be simple, either unconditional or conditioned on a few very clear and broad contingencies. Such rules must strike a balance between the opposing considerations of commitment and flexibility.

There does exist a halfway house that combines some of the simplicity with some of the advantages of both commitment and flexibility. This is to use an unconditional rule at some times, keep flexibility at others, and to define threshold levels of contingencies at which the policy would switch from one regime to the other. For example, consider a country whose equilibrium real exchange rate fluctuates vis-à-vis the rest of the world because of random shocks to productivity, and whose government has the temptation to pull inflation surprises. Commitment to a nominal exchange rate can control the latter, but flexibility is needed to adjust to the former. So long as the real exchange rate is not too far out of equilibrium, the commitment advantage is more important; but when there is a severe disequilibrium, flexibility has more value. Suppose the country can switch from one regime to the other by incurring a lump-sum up-front (sunk) cost. This cost may consist of the time and political effort needed for legislation, starting a new agency or institution to implement the new regime, acquiring a reputation, and even more important, when there is ongoing uncertainty, an option value of preserving the status quo in case the situation reverses itself without the government taking any costly action. This last component is similar to the option value that arises in models of irreversible investment. Then a switch from the commitment regime to the flexible regime should be made when the disequilibrium becomes so large, and the net advantage of flexibility over commitment grows so large, that it provides a sufficient rate of return on the sunk lump-sum cost of switching. The reverse switch should be made when the disequilibrium is small enough to justify that move using a similar calculation. There will be a range between these thresholds where the current regime should be maintained.

Haubrich and Ritter (1995) have developed this idea more formally; an earlier analysis which considered only one switch rather than ongoing uncertainty was in Lohmann 1992. The full characterization of the optimal thresholds requires a dynamic programming model, and the correct calculation of the option value of the status quo can get quite difficult, but the idea is simple and intuitive, as are the results.

Figure 2.1 gives a schematic illustration of the point. The horizontal axis measures the difference between the real exchange rate and its equilibrium level. At any instant the state of the economy is represented by a point along this line. The exogenous shocks that affect the economy affect either the actual real exchange rate or the equilibrium rate, thereby altering the amount of disequilibrium. Thus the economy moves as a stochastic process on this line.

The vertical axis shows the annual value of the net advantage of commitment over flexibility. The immediate value of real output can be raised by changing the exchange rate, and this benefit of flexibility is greater, the larger the disequilibrium in absolute value. The benefit of commitment is the value of its reputational capital, for example, the knowledge that the government will not use its freedom to inflate the economy, at least for some time to come. This value is greater, the closer the exchange rate is to its equilibrium level. Therefore, the balance favors commitment when the amount of disequilibrium is small and favors flexibility when the disequilibrium is large. Therefore, the curve relating the net advantage of commitment to the level of disequilibrium has an inverse

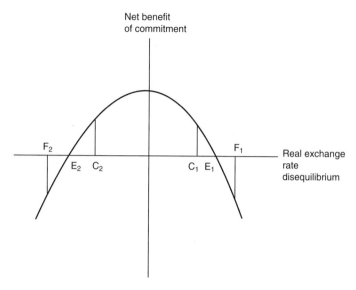

Figure 2.1
Optimal switches between commitment and flexibility

U-shape.[6] The curve is shown crossing zero at the points E_1
and E_2, respectively, in the positive and negative directions.
   When should the regime be switched from commitment
to flexibility and vice versa? The answer depends on the
stochastic process of the disequilibrium and the costs of
switching regimes, but one thing is clear: switches should
not be made as soon as the points E_1 or E_2 are crossed. The
reason is that each switch incurs a sunk cost, which cannot
be recouped if the stochastic process reverses itself in the
near future. This creates the option value of waiting to see
if the stochastic shock is persistent. Switches are optimally

6. The relationship need not in general be symmetric for positive and negative amounts of disequilibrium because overvaluation and undervalua-
tion affect economic performance in different ways.

made only when the per period advantage of the alternative regime has become sufficiently large, and not merely positive. The figure assumes such calculations have been done, and shows the outcome. If the economy is initially in the commitment regime, and crosses F_1 from left to right or F_2 from right to left (both cases correspond to increasing disequilibrium), it should switch to the flexible regime. If it is initially in the flexible regime and crosses C_1 from right to left or C_2 from left to right (both cases correspond to shrinking disequilibrium), it should switch to the commitment regime. Thus, to the right of F_1 or to the left of F_2 it should always be in the flexible regime; in the range between C_1 and C_2 it should always be in the commitment regime; and in the ranges $C_1 F_1$ and $C_2 F_2$ the current regime, whichever it may be, should continue. The points E_1 and E_2, where the flow advantage of the two regimes is equal, lie in these ranges where inaction is optimal, but it is not optimal to switch as soon as E_1 or E_2 is crossed.

This analysis says nothing about who makes the switch and how the initial constitution that provides for these switches can ensure that they will be made at the optimal thresholds, rather than too soon (because costs of switching are not recognized or are borne by some other agency of the government, or the option value of the status quo is forgotten), or too late (because the agency in charge of the current regime miscalculates, or finds it in its own special interests to minimize the advantage of the switch and holds on too long). In other words, although the constitution may give us a rule that mandates a switch, in practice the switch is a policy act, with its attendant transaction costs, so it may occur in a way different from that stipulated by the constitutional rule. Different countries and institutions succeed in resolving this dilemma to different extents and in different ways. This reminds us once again that constitutions are incomplete contracts, and the distinction between them and policy acts is one of degree, not kind. The same remarks apply more generally to all the devices of commitment and delegation; the political process can always rescind them, albeit at a cost.

Repetition and Reputation

Bilateral Trade is more important.

The emergence of cooperation through repetition of plays in games like the Prisoners' Dilemma has long been known in game theory. The general idea is that a player may secure a short-run advantage by deviating from the action that the mutually beneficial cooperative regime requires of him, but the deviation carries a future cost, namely, a lower payoff for himself as others also deviate, either because the cooperation collapses in a general way, or because the others deliberately punish one's initial deviation. This idea has been built into some very elaborate theoretical models that specify more precisely the information and the actions available to the participants, determine the equilibrium of the resulting repeated game, and thereby help us understand which forces are conducive to the sustainment of cooperation and which ones are destructive of it. To give a very crude summary, cooperation is more likely (1) the longer the horizon of the relationship, (2) the more patient the players, in the sense that they do not discount future payoffs too much in relation to immediate ones, (3) the more quickly and more accurately a deviation is detected, and (4) the higher the cost inflicted by the punishment on the initial deviator (A thorough treatment of this theory is in Fudenberg and Tirole 1991, chapters 4, 5).

A closely related but somewhat different way to think of this idea is in terms of reputation. In a repeated relationship, each participant can stand to benefit by acquiring and preserving a reputation concerning his future actions. Thus a government can secure a better outcome for the economy if it has a reputation for not confiscating private-sector capital at will, which leads to more private investment and therefore to growth. This reputation can be thought of as any other valuable capital asset: building it up and maintaining it entails a short-run cost, and running it down or failing to maintain it gets some short-run benefit. If the future is long enough or important enough, such short-run temptations can be resisted.

Reputation has an aspect that goes beyond mere repetition, namely, that of incomplete information. The private sector typically has no direct way of knowing whether a government is truly determined to keep inflation low and therefore has an incentive to establish a reputation to this effect. As is usual in these matters, actions speak louder than words. Therefore the government may need to signal its determination by being excessively zealous for a while in its pursuit of low inflation. And a government that is in fact weaker in its resolve may find it desirable to get the economic benefits of low inflation by mimicking the actions of a stronger type. Fudenberg and Tirole (1991, chapter 9) discuss these issues in detail.

If the forces of repetition or reputation are strong enough, no explicit commitment technology is needed to secure commitment; the policymakers' own incentives ensure that they will not be tempted to deviate from the commitment. This idea has been developed furthest in the literature on macroeconomic (monetary and fiscal) policies. The introduction and several articles in Persson and Tabellini 1994a discuss these issues in detail and depth. Effects of ongoing relationships between rival political parties are examined by Moe (1990). He points out that the power to govern, or to exercise public authority, is a kind of property right, and in a democracy this is uncertain. Each party will try, not only to achieve the policies it wants, but also to prevent the opposition from overturning them totally should it come into power. In an ongoing relationship, the solution from the parties' perspective consists of political compromise. Policies that are enacted, and bureaucracies that are formed to implement them, embody some concessions to the current losers. These can include fragmented authority, checks and balances, delays, and procedures that give the opposition opportunities to participate and influence the results. Moe argues that the result is delay, ineffectiveness, and failure of decisionmaking. Laffont and Tirole (1993, chapter 16) and Tirole (1994, p. 17) also observe that political uncertainty stops governments from committing policies for the long term, but they argue that if the government in power at any time is likely to be biased toward a particular group, letting it lock in policies that favor this group may be socially detrimental, so the checks and balances serve a good purpose.

In international trade politics, Prisoners' Dilemmas are frequent. Liberal or open trade regimes are in the mutual interest of all countries jointly, but each has a private incentive to deviate in various ways: (1) to levy import tariffs to exploit its monopoly power in trade and improve its terms of trade, (2) to restrict imports or promote exports to give its firms a strategic advantage in industries characterized by international oligopoly, and (3) to satisfy the demands of its domestic protectionist pressure groups.

An organization like the General Agreement on Tariffs and
Trade (GATT) or its successor, the World Trade Organization (WTO), can assist in the resolution of such dilemmas,
by sanctioning punishment against deviators. In practice
the ability of these organizations to assist has been limited,
because the sanctions available to them have been limited,
slow, and uncertain.

The early theoretical literature on these issues was surveyed by Dixit (1987); numerous more recent developments
are discussed by Staiger (1995). Here I will touch on just a
few that involve transaction costs most prominently. My
discussion is based on Staiger's.

For simplicity of exposition, consider a group of countries that are symmetrically related to each other, for example in the overall size of the economy and that of the export
sectors of each, and ignore each country's internal politics.
Let $U(T, t)$ denote each country's social welfare during one
period, say a year, when its tariff rate is T and that of each
of the other countries is t. A single-period, noncooperative
Nash equilibrium t_0 is that rate which is the best for each
country when all the others are using it, too. Formally, it is
defined by the fixed-point problem:

$$T = t_0 \text{ maximizes } U(T, t_0).$$

Now consider the group in a repeated interaction, trying
to sustain a cooperative common tariff rate t less than t_0.
Each country has the temptation to cheat and levy its own
optimal higher tariff rate in reponse to the others' t. It can
get away with this for only one period; thereafter, cooperation will collapse, and the situation will revert to repeated
Nash play of t_0. Each country, in deciding whether to cheat,
must balance the immediate gain against the future loss
from so doing.

The benefit of cheating is given by

$$B(t) = \max_{T} U(T,t) - U(t,t).$$

The cost of cheating is the capitalized value, at the appropriate interest rate r, of the drop in social welfare in going from the cooperative to the Nash outcome:

$$C(t) = [U(t,t) - U(t_0,t_0)]/r.$$

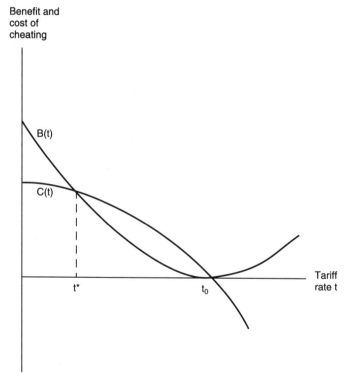

Benefit and
cost of
cheating

B(t)

C(t)

t*

t_0

Tariff
rate t

Figure 2.2
Cooperation in repeated tariff game

These functions are shown in Figure 2.2. If the countries are not trying to sustain anything other than the noncooperative Nash tariff level t_0, the benefit to one country from cheating is zero, as is the cost of cheating. Thus $B(t_0) = 0$ and $C(t_0) = 0$. Away from t_0, the benefit $B(t)$ rises on either side, and it is a convex function of t because the farther away from the one-shot equilibrium the current situation, the more can one country gain by its deviation. $C(t)$ is a decreasing function, because the higher the current common level of the tariff, the less will one country be hurt by reversion to t_0. (If the current t is for some reason higher than t_0, then it will actually gain, so $C(t)$ is negative to the right of t_0, but that is not an economically relevant part of the picture.) Since free trade is collectively optimal, $U(t, t)$ is maximized at $t = 0$; that is why the $C(t)$ curve is horizontal where it meets the vertical axis.

The $C(t)$ curve could stay above the $B(t)$ curve throughout the range $(0, t_0)$; then any cooperative arrangement to reduce tariffs would be self-sustaining because for each member country the cost of cheating would be higher than the benefit. The figure shows a more interesting case where the two curves intersect at a positive t^* to the left of t_0. In the range (t^*, t_0), the cost of deviation is greater than the benefit, so any tariff in this range is sustainable as a cooperative equilibrium of the repeated game. In particular, t^* is the lowest tariff (most cooperation) that can be so sustained.

The most important general idea conveyed by this analysis is just this limit on the feasibility of mutually beneficial cooperation. When no outside authority can enforce a cooperative agreement, attempting too much may give each member too great a temptation. In such a world, if we see the group of countries seeking more liberal trade but stopping short of complete free trade, we should not regard that as a political failure. Given the very real transaction costs — enforcement problems — they face, they may be doing the best they can. In Williamson's terminology, if the countries fail to achieve a cooperative tariff rate of less than t^*, this is not remediable. However, if they settle on a rate that exceeds t^*, then that is remediable because agreement on a tariff rate equal to t^* is feasible.

The benefit and cost curves are determined by many things, including the rate at which the future is discounted, the accuracy and the delay with which deviations are observed, and by other possibly observable circumstances like economic booms or depressions. The above account leaves out all these details, but we can understand their effects by considering how they will shift the two curves. Here are just a few of these considerations.

If the future is discounted more heavily, then $C(t)$, which is a discounted present value of future costs, is reduced in magnitude. Therefore the intersection t^* shifts to the right — less cooperation can be sustained. It is commonly believed that politicians have extremely short time horizons, and that the policy process operates with extremely high discount rates. Most governments, especially democratic ones, are under pressure from the media, the opposition, and the public and are supposed to look for results demonstrable before the next election. Former British Prime Minister Harold Wilson's famous remark, "A week is a long time in politics," is an even more extreme statement of the same belief. Therefore repetition as a way of sustaining cooperation in policy games seems questionable. However, the political process can sometimes take a longer view, and major trade agreements seem to be such occasions. When ratification of various GATT rounds comes up, a concerted effort is usually made by diplomats, some media, and academics to remind the public as well as politicians of the long term. Even then short-term arguments in favor of protection do arise, and they keep on arising with greater force in the interim years between these major economy-wide negotiating rounds, as particular industries keep on confronting new trade-related problems.

If detecting cooperation becomes harder or slower, then $B(t)$ rises and again less cooperation can be sustained. Some observers of the GATT have claimed that its dispute-settlement procedures, by placing the onus to start them on the country that was hurt by another country's trade-restricting deviation, speeded up the detection of such deviations. However, the subsequent process—convening a panel, holding hearings, issuing a ruling, and subjecting it to a vote where the culpable country had an effective veto power—was slow and uncertain.

If countries can be made to feel some larger obligation to the international community, then a "psychic cost" adds to $C(t)$ and increases the range of possible cooperation. This may seem a slender thread to the economist, but some observers in trade law assert that this had some effect.

More subtle, the world is not stationary but is subject to various economic fluctuations. If one country is suffering from a depression, or is subjected to a sudden surge of imports that hurts some domestic groups particularly severely, this temporarily raises the benefit, economic or political, that it can gain from reneging on its trade agreements. This can lead to a collapse of the whole agreement. A wise system will anticipate this and allow for deviations in response to some clearly observed circumstances of this kind. Thus, a country may be allowed to raise tariffs temporarily in response to some clearly defined circumstances without triggering a trade war. GATT's "escape clause" or "safe-guards" can be thought of as designed to serve exactly this purpose. Bagwell and Staiger (1990) developed this idea.

Another issue in international politics where repetition and reputation have been claimed to play a role is that of sovereign debt. In the absence of effective international laws that enforce the collection of a national government's obligations to foreign creditors, such lending will take place only if there are effective mechanisms based on the government's own incentive to service or repay its debts. The idea is that the cost of collapse of the agreement, namely, inability to borrow again in the future, could keep the country repaying its past debts. However, as Bulow and Rogoff (1989) have pointed out, this is not enough. A sovereign debt contract can be sustained as an equilibrium of a repeated game only if the discounted present value of the country's future repayment streams is *always* nonpositive. If there ever were a future time and state of the world where the country saw itself making positive present-value repayments, it could default and use this sum instead as the initial collateral for other transactions that will allow it to do better. Therefore the system needs some other enforcement power, for example, the ability to seize the defaulting country's trade or assets.

More generally, this analysis suggests another weakness of mechanisms based purely on repetition and reputation: they are vulnerable to renegotiation. The defaulting country could in effect say to its creditors: "I reneged on the old loan, but that is a bygone, and we should not let it spoil the mutually profitable future opportunities that exist for us." As long as some future potential lenders can be tempted by this, the cost to the country of the initial default is reduced. The initial lenders can anticipate all this, so the ongoing relationship may never get started. Game theory has examined how some cooperation can be salvaged despite the possibility of renegotiation, but the results so far are not very encouraging.

2.3.2   Commitments in Practice

The above theoretical analysis of commitments was accompanied by some examples of their use in practice, but there are other examples worth mention. Commitment devices that restrict ex post opportunistic freedom of action are legion in political constitutions as well as policy acts. The U.S. Constitution and the Bill of Rights are full of them: "No title of nobility shall be granted by the United States"; "No tax or duty shall be levied on articles exported from any State"; "Congress shall make no law respecting an establishment of religion, or prohibiting the free exercise thereof; or abridging the freedom of speech, or of the press; or the right of the people peaceably to assemble, and to petition the Government for a redress of grievances"; and perhaps most important in the context of economic policy, "No bill of attainder or ex post facto law shall be passed." Such constitutional commitments are generally very firm and subject to very few ad hoc exceptions, probably because they are enforced by an independent judiciary that sees just this task as its mission. Even then there are some loopholes, particularly instances of retroactive taxation that are allowed despite the provision barring "ex post facto laws."

In electoral politics, the proposal for term limits that is currently gaining support in the United States can be seen as making a commitment to avoid a future temptation. The electorate as a whole fears the abuse of powers by long-lived professional politicians, but each local constituency gets "addicted" to its own representative because of the benefits a politician with seniority in Washington, D.C. can bring to his or her district. All citizens can collectively agree to avoid this temptation to reelect their own congressman or senator by committing themselves in advance to a term limit. Of course there are other arguments both for and against this proposal, and the commitment aspect must be weighed against the others.

Regulatory Agencies
The U.S. Congress often creates independent agencies to make economic decisions on their merits and on a nonpolitical basis, and to use their expertise and information to respond promptly and flexibly to new demands on policy than a more centralized political institution could. The independence of the agencies creates some new questions: How can these agencies be protected from capture by the very interests they are supposed to regulate, and from behaving arbitrarily in other ways? The Congress's typical solution is to impose constraints on the actions of the agencies. These often lead to micromanagement by Congress and the reentry of politics. Thus the commitments are imperfect and only partially successful in achieving their stated aims, and they introduce new potential problems. These ideas are developed and illustrated in Noll 1989, pp. 1278–1281, McCubbins, Noll, and Weingast 1987, Wilson 1989, pp. 242–243, and Levy and Spiller 1994.

Noll examines and illustrates the mechanisms of political control that restrain such agencies. These include appointment power, control of the agency's budget, and direct requirements such as those under the Environmental Protection Act and the Occupational Safety and Health

Act. The relationship between constraints and incentives as alternative methods of controlling agencies was discussed earlier (see also McCubbins, Noll, and Weingast 1987 and Spiller 1990). A related problem is to ensure stability in the policy followed by the agency. If potential investors in a regulated industry have reason to fear that the returns to their investments will be expropriated by future regulatory actions, for example, price ceilings will be imposed in response to consumer concerns, they will be reluctant to make such investments. The outcome will be undesirable, even from the point of view of the consumers. Therefore it is important to put in place mechanisms that can restrain such arbitrariness. Levy and Spiller (1994) discuss the role of the judiciary in this. They find that all the countries in their sample where regulatory systems have successfully constrained the arbitrary exercise of power to the detriment of investment have "independent and well regarded" judiciaries with "a record of hearing regulatory disputes and resolving them impartially." However, they find many other variations in these countries' systems. Thus there need be no one clear route to success in coping with transaction costs; answers can be specific to the context.

Krueger's (1990) study of the evolution of the United States' sugar trade barriers and price support policies shows how programs acquire a life of their own. Shifts of the underlying economic interests concerning sugar, and diplomatic issues involving sugar-producing countries, led to major shifts in the intent, the mechanisms, and the effects of that program. Commitments in the form of laws and institutions that were made for one purpose ended up serving quite new and different purposes. For example, quotas were instituted and allocated in the late 1940s to help the Cuban economy and United States investors' interests in Cuba. After 1960 import restrictions were retained to serve the interests of U.S. domestic growers and other sweetener manufacturers, and the import quotas were reallocated to other countries that were friendly to the United States.

Monetary Policy
Much theoretical work on monetary policy has found that an independent central bank is an important commitment device to prevent inflation. In practice, in most countries the central bank has traditionally functioned under varying degrees of control from the treasury. The German Bundesbank is perhaps the closest one finds to the ideal independent central bank with a clear anti-inflation mandate. In the United States the Federal Reserve has a lot of independence, but is not immune to political pressures.

Several empirical researchers have found evidence from cross-country data that a greater degree of central bank independence is associated with a lower average rate of inflation and less volatility of inflation (see the discussion in Persson and Tabellini 1994, pp. 20–21). In recent years the theoretical and empirical arguments seem to have had some effect, and more countries have begun to work toward giving greater independence to their central banks.

Fiscal Policy
In budgetary matters, a rule or a constitutional amendment requiring balance is often proposed as a way to curb the temptation of Congress to push the costs of current expenditures on to future generations. Most analysts recognize this to be a weak device. The "balanced budget" is only a forecast, and it can be fudged with rosy scenarios and

assumptions. There are also many explicit loopholes in all such proposals. Many of these devices are exposed in Cogan, Muris, and Schick 1994. These served to undermine the deficit-cutting commitment of the Gramm-Rudman-Hollings Act of 1985, and may also do the same to the "pay-as-you-go" provisions of the Budget Enforcement Act of 1990; these are discussed in more detail in the next chapter.

The "pay-as-you-go" provision had an unintended effect that illustrates that commitments have potentially harmful or costly side effects. The tariff cuts agreed to in the GATT Uruguay Round (leading to the new World Trade Organization [WTO]) are estimated to cost about $14 billion in lost revenues over the next five years. Under the provisions of the act, this must be compensated for by a tax increase or cuts in other entitlement expenditures. The first proved difficult in the prevailing political climate; as for the second, every particular entitlement has its group of beneficiaries who are vocal and strong in resisting any cuts. The resulting impasse threatened ratification of the whole GATT-WTO agreement in the Congress, and indeed, interests opposed to the GATT and the WTO latched on to this issue to achieve their aims. In the end a loophole came to the rescue; the pay-as-you-go provision could be waived with the support of sixty senators, and this was achieved.

In trade matters, the United States' fast-track procedures are an example of a commitment that has on the whole been successful. Here, the U.S. Congress commits itself to a procedure whereby it will vote on domestic legislation implementing international trade agreements in an expedited manner—limited debate, no amendments, and a simple up-or-down vote. Without such a deal, other countries would hesitate to negotiate with the United States, for fear that the Congress would take the agreement as merely the starting point of new de facto negotiations and attempt to extract further concessions. Gilligan and Krehbiel (1987) offer an informational explanation for such "closed rules." Most new legislation is complex and requires much information gathering; this task is assigned to small standing committees. The committees would not expend this effort if the whole legislature could use the information and then pick apart the committee proposals. A rule restricting amendments serves as the commitment device that gets around this problem and ensures better-informed legislation. In the context of trade negotiations, the fast-track procedure similarly serves to ensure good-faith negotiation. The arrangement has lasted, albeit not without controversy, for almost sixty years, but its continuation is once again in doubt.

Finally, many countries, particularly less-developed ones, in need of fiscal and monetary restraint are able to make a commitment by using international organizations such as the World Bank or the International Monetary Fund as "delegates" for this purpose. When their domestic constituents press for protection, subsidies, or inflationary finance, the treasuries can point to the conditions imposed by these bodies in return for much-needed project loans or foreign currency. Thus the countries' governments can escape the blame while pursuing policies that many of them would agree to be in the national interest anyway.

2.3.3   Agency and Incentives   *Monitoring*

Next I consider the class of transaction costs that arise because of information asymmetries, where one party to the transaction does not know another's attributes, such as skill or tastes (adverse selection), or cannot observe another's actions, such as effort (moral hazard). In the context of economic policy, agents (government bureaucrats, regulators, executive departments) possess such information advantage over the principals (voters, lobbyists, politicians). Some of these problems can be partly resolved by better efforts of monitoring, and by indirect tax instruments that have some effect on the actions of the participants (see Arnott and Stiglitz 1989 and Greenwald and Stiglitz 1986). However, the tax instruments cause distortions elsewhere in the economy, and many information asymmetries remain after such instruments have been used. The economist's standard and more direct answer to such problems is to design an appropriate incentive scheme.

In the case of adverse selection, the agent must be given a sufficient share of the economic surplus or rent that exists in the relationship in order to reveal truthfully the information he possesses. If the information is a continuous variable, for example the agent's skill level, then a schedule linking rent to information must be constructed to offer the right marginal incentive to reveal each increment of favorable information. This need to give away rent is a cost to the principal; therefore he does not push its use to the full extent that would be first-best in a hypothetical world of full information, and the agent's skill is underutilized. This is the social cost of the information asymmetry. I will discuss these incentive schemes in more detail later.

In the case of moral hazard, the problem is the need to balance risk and incentive. The typical situation is one where the principal has a much greater ability to bear risk than the agent. If information is symmetric, the agent can be given a fixed sum in return for providing a specified effort. Such a contract can combine optimal effort and risk bearing. If the agent's effort cannot be publicly observed (and often the quality of effort is impossible to observe), this first-best solution is infeasible.

Still, if the agent is risk-neutral, then the principal can give him the rights to make decisions in return for a fixed fee, thus in effect selling the whole operation. The agent, facing the full consequences of his own effort, will achieve the first-best by setting his effort at a level where the marginal reward to effort equals its marginal cost. We say that the incentive scheme implicit in full ownership is very *high-powered;* at the margin it gives the agent 100 percent of value.

If the agent is risk-averse, then the desirability of sharing risk will lower the power of the incentive scheme. The principal will give the agent some sure income and less than 100 percent of marginal value. This will dampen the agent's incentive to exert effort, and the outcome will be a second-best with too little effort relative to the first-best above. However, the unobservability of the effort (the information asymmetry) being a fact of the situation, this is an unavoidable cost. The limitation cannot be wished away, and the ideal first-best, or the outcome that *could* be achieved if the agent's effort *were* observable and the contract *could* specify the amount and quality of effort the agent was required to exert, has no operational significance. We can only ask if the parties are coping with the information asymmetry as best as they can, that is, whether they are achieving a second-best.

The political process of making economic policy, and the administrative process of implementing it, have their own information asymmetries. Bureaucratic agencies have and acquire specialized information, and they can vary the quality and quantity of their efforts in ways that are largely unobservable to outsiders. The firms and the public, whose actions the policy is trying to affect, have their own private information and actions that they can manipulate so as to secure greater advantage from the policy or to mitigate adverse effects of it. We might therefore begin to think of appropriately designed incentive schemes. However, it is often found that the incentives in such situations are very low-powered; instead, the government agencies are subjected to various constraints (Wilson 1989, p. 115). I will examine some analyses of incentives in the theory of economic policy and then return to this question of low power.

The theory is most developed on the subject of influencing the actions of an agent who possesses some pertinent information that is not known to the policy-maker. Such situations are ubiquitous in the making and carrying out of economic policy. When a government chooses an income tax schedule, or regulates the pricing of power or transportation services, it needs information that is in the hands of those—firms, consumers, and taxpayers—who are influenced by these policies. They will typically benefit by misrepresenting their information; the taxpayers can understate their earnings potential, and the firms can inflate their costs. This constrains the feasible and optimal policies. The general principle is that the agent must be given some of the rent or the economic surplus that exists in the transaction in order to induce him to take an action that directly or indirectly reveals his information. Thus a taxpayer who utilizes his productive potential must be allowed to keep enough of the extra income he generates; a firm that reveals its low cost or superior technology must be allowed enough profit to make it worth its while to do so. This idea goes back to Mirrlees's 1971 article on optimal nonlinear income taxation, was formalized into a general theorem (the Revelation Principle) by Myerson (1979) and others, and applied to the problem of regulating a firm with unknown cost by Baron and Myerson (1982). It has spawned a very large literature on the theory of regulation, including many subtleties that arise when the interaction between the policymaker and the regulated firm lasts for a long time, when the firm produces several outputs or can vary its product quality, and so on. The same theory also offers solution to the problems of designing auctions of natural resource deposits, other public assets that can be used in private production, and so on. Laffont and Tirole 1993 is a thorough and masterly treatment of this theory; Armstrong, Cowan and Vickers 1994, chapters 2, 3 gives a compact but valuable exposition.

Relative to the large volume of theory, practical uses of such schemes in actual policymaking seem very rare. This is not to say that incentive issues are ignored in actual regulatory policy. Although regulation originated in the more classical normative concern about market failures, particularly the market power possessed by providers of public services, issues of information and incentive quickly assumed prominence. In the United States, regulation of power utilities and telecommunications that allowed the firms a "fair" rate of return was found to lead to padding or shifting of costs into the base on which this return was calculated. In practice the policy often took the form of a price cap that was adjusted every so often for inflation and a predetermined productivity factor. This method was most formally adopted in the United Kingdom (see Armstrong, Cowan, and Vickers 1994, chapters 6–10 for a discussion). In the United States, similar practices were adopted by the Federal Communications Commission (FCC) in the late

1980s and by several state regulatory agencies soon thereafter (see Joskow and Schmalensee 1986 for a detailed and
insightful examination of the U.S. practices in regulation
of electric utilities). In practice such schemes do not work
perfectly. The initial price cap is set on the basis of costs,
and subsequent adjustments allow "renegotiation" if prof-
its turn out to be too high or too low; that brings back
the link with costs and hence some of the problems of the
rate-of-return regulation.

Economists' advice did play an important part in improving the practice of incentive regulation, but it was
mostly based on simple economic intuitions such as the
need to detach prices from costs to provide incentives to
reduce costs, or temporal price discrimination to smooth
production, rather than any of the the advanced theoretical
research on incentive (see Joskow and Noll 1981, which
predates the advent of modern information economics).
The closest today's sophisticated incentive theory comes to
practice is probably the menu of contracts offered by the
FCC to U.S. regional Bell operating companies, where they
can choose between a low price cap and a high share of
earnings, or the other way round. Then the more efficient
firms have the incentive to reveal this by picking the former, and the less efficient firms the latter; this corresponds
to the theory in Laffont and Tirole 1993, chapter 2.

A similar lack of contact between theory and practice can
be found in a conceptually related area of economic policy, namely, eliciting people's willingness to pay for public
goods. When nonpayers cannot be excluded from enjoy-
ing the benefits of such goods, every individual has the
incentive to become a free rider on the sacrifice of others;
when all conceal their willingness to pay in this way, the
good does not get supplied at all. Economists have devised

extremely clever rules of operation, or mechanisms, under which truthful revelation of willingness to pay becomes optimal (see Vickrey 1961, Clarke 1971, and Groves and Ledyard 1977). Similar schemes have been devised to deal with externalities; a particularly good example is Sinn's (1993) idea of combining incentive aspects with the traditional Pigovian taxation to control environmental pollution. Another appealing theoretical contribution is Varian's (1994) two-stage scheme for implementing an efficient solution when individuals causing mutual externalities know one another's valuation of these externalities, but the policymaker does not.

Some research experiments have been conducted to examine the performance of such schemes, and some uses have been attempted in small group settings like the allocation of budgets for public television programs (see Davis and Holt 1993, chapter 6). Probably the best-known scheme of this kind in actual use is the National Intern Matching Program for entry-level physicians and U.S. hospitals (see Roth 1984 and Roth and Sotomayor 1990). This program evolved out of trial and experience and was only later analyzed by economic theorists for its incentive properties. Other than these, I have not been able to find any instances of uses of such schemes in the numerous actual contexts where decisions concerning public goods are made.

An important recent instance where economic theorists played a significant role in designing the procedures of an incentive scheme is the auction of broadcasting-spectrum rights in the United States. McMillan (1994) gives an account of the early phases of this ongoing story. Ironically, the available theory of auctions does not formally treat the complexity of the actual auctions; the theorists who participated in the process were supplementing simpler formal models with general economic intuition. The reason for resort to the auction process, too, probably has little to do with economics. The auctions of spectrum bands for personal communications systems (PCS) raised over $8 billion; those for high-definition digital television (HDTV), and for the spectrum bands that become free as a result of the advent of this more efficient system of television broadcasting, promise to raise even more revenue. In the present times of budgetary restraint, this is an important attraction of auctions. This, rather than any concern for allocative efficiency, may lead to more widespread use of auctions of public resources, replacing the previous practice of giving them away on the basis of political criteria. Politics retains a role in the auctions, however; the PCS auctions included special treatment for small businesses or minority-owned businesses, and there is ongoing debate about what use restrictions to place on the winners of any future HDTV auctions.

The divergence between theoretical advances and policy practices can be explained in several ways. First, some of the theory of incentives is too complex to explain to the regulators and the public; simple price caps are easier to understand. Second, even though the theory has become quite rich in its treatment of multiproduct firms, dynamics, and so forth, reality is more complex still. As Joskow and Schmalensee (1986, p. 24) point out, the theory has "not produced a neat set of cookbook rules that can be readily applied," and "no single incentive scheme will be optimal in all circumstances." These two hurdles can be overcome in due course as the theory improves and its exposition is simplified. But a third obstacle is perhaps the most important and harder to surmount. This is the fact that regulation is a profoundly political process, not the exercise of dictatorship by a single principal—whether or not informationally constrained, and whether or not benevolent—that the economic theory of the subject has traditionally assumed. And all the interested parties like the political process. The regulators use the hearing process as a way to gather information; the regulated firms and consumer advocates both think that they will help themselves and influence regulators better by making their arguments in an open forum.

In other words, the pervasive mode of regulation in political economy is a *common agency* where multiple principals simultaneously try to influence the agent. I will argue later that the equilibrium of the game between these principals will typically be characterized by very low-powered incentives. For similar reasons, the multiplicity of principals may make it impossible to implement the theoretically efficient information-revealing schemes.

Finally, I should mention some models of macroeconomic politics that explain the relation of economic cycles and elections in terms of information problems and incentive structures. Early studies of such "political business cycles" deriving from Nordhaus (1975) simply assumed that the government's chances of reelection would be increased if it engineered a boom as the election approached. This is not logically satisfactory because it assumes that the public is taken in by this blatant ploy. However, if the public cannot directly observe the government's effort and therefore rewards the observable outcome, namely, the economy's performance (Ferejohn 1986) or if the public does not know the competence of the incumbent government and takes the economy's performance as a signal of it (Rogoff 1990), such cycles can be explained in a rigorous game-theoretic equilibrium framework. These papers are reprinted, and the general issue is discussed in the introduction to Persson and Tabellini 1994b.

2.3.4 The Low Power of Incentives in Policymaking

The brief review above dealt with incentive schemes that can be implemented by a benevolent dictator to elicit some information or effort from private firms and consumers in an attempt to implement a better economic outcome. Incentive schemes can influence the information and actions of the political or administrative institutions themselves. These differ from corresponding schemes that we see in private economic transactions in some important ways: the rewards or penalties are often nonmonetary, and the incentives are often low-powered.

Even in economic contexts, rewards or penalties may be financial or nonmonetary. The former category must be interpreted broadly to include career concerns, that is, future material rewards as well as the immediate payoff; similarly, a broad interpretation of nonmonetary incentives includes status, power, and job satisfaction. In political contexts the nonfinancial aspects are likely to be more important than in economics. Even with this understanding, however, it is commonly observed that incentives for policymakers are quite low-powered; the marginal rewards for producing an outcome of greater value to society, or the marginal penalties for doing worse, are generally a very low percentage of the value added or lost. A bureaucrat in the Office of Management and Budget, or an international trade negotiator, can take actions that benefit or hurt the economy to the tune of billions of dollars, but the effect on his own compensation, monetary or otherwise, is at most a very tiny fraction of this. Much of the commonly held belief that political processes and institutions cope poorly with agency problems can be attributed to the low power of their incentives. Previous analysts have offered several reasons for this; I will now review them and add another that seems to me to be of even greater importance.

The discussion can be organized by reference to Wilson's (1989) excellent observations about agency relationships in government bureaucracies. He identifies two key features: (1) Government bureaucracies typically have several dimensions of effort (input) and result (output), and each of these is only imperfectly observable or verifiable (pp. 129–131); (2) each agency deals with several "principals" who are simultaneously trying to influence its decisions — the executive and legislative branches of government, the courts, interest groups, media, and so on (pp. 236–237, 300). Wilson argues that, as a result, the principals impose a variety of constraints on the agency, instead of the kind of powerful incentive schemes that are more commonly suggested in economic agency problems (pp. 115, 125, 133, 332). The outcome, according to Wilson, is that government agencies can stop things from happening but find it difficult to get anything positive done (p. 317). Wilson's argument is informal, but sufficiently intriguing to be worth formal exploration using the modern theories of multitask and common agencies.

Multitask Agencies
Holmström and Milgrom (1991) have developed a model of multitask agencies that helps us understand some of the features of government agencies stressed by Wilson. The agent has to perform several tasks, which are at least

partly competing for the agent's attention and effort. The agency's priorities over these tasks do not coincide with those of the principal, perhaps because they require different qualities of effort, or because new tasks have less value to the agency in terms of its original mission. In any case, the principal must devise an incentive scheme to alter the effort allocation of the agent. The choice will depend on the degree of observability of different inputs and outputs, as well as on the differences in values between the two parties. Holmström and Milgrom find two important results. First, if the result of one task is very poorly observable, then the incentive scheme for a competing task must have lower power in order to avoid excessive diversion of effort away from this task to more observable ones. Second, if some tasks are primarily of value to the agent, and can be controlled in an all-or-nothing fashion, then it may be desirable for the principal to simply prohibit these, rather than try to give extra incentives for others. This point is especially important if the incentives for other tasks must be low-powered in conformity with the first result.

An example close to home will make the point clear. University professors have two tasks, teaching and research. The output of research is relatively easily measurable in terms of prestigious publication and citations; that of teaching is more nebulous because the real effects are long term, and the students' evaluations have their own biases. If the university considered each task and its incentives in isolation, it would recognize the different precisions of information and set up a high-powered reward scheme for research and a low-powered one for teaching; but that would induce professors to divert effort away from teaching and into research. Therefore, considering the two together, the university is forced to reduce the power of its scheme for rewarding research, too.[7]

Now introduce a third activity, outside consulting, that is primarily of value to the professor rather than to the university. If the reward schemes for teaching *and* research are low-powered for the reasons explained above, then teachers will divert their effort into consulting. The university could cope with this by increasing the power of the incentives for teaching and research together, but that is a costly alternative because teaching effort is not easily observable. (The reward must be based on observables such as students' performance or their evaluations of the teaching; therefore teachers may get rewarded for their luck in having better students, or for gimmicks that appeal to students and raise the evaluations without really improving the quality of the education.) The university therefore instead prohibits consulting, or at least restricts the time allowed for it. Some consulting will be allowed if that makes it easier to ensure that the professor gets enough utility from the whole bundle of activities to be willing to work for the university, that is, to satisfy the professor's individual rationality (participation) constraint. But this calculation will involve comparing the average product of consulting time and the marginal reward for teaching and research. A full social optimum would equate the marginal products of the two. This departure from the ideal is the unavoidable cost of the information asymmetry in this case.

---

7. A better solution may be greater specialization among universities. Some can place more emphasis and reward on research, while others concentrate on teaching; then, each will attract the type of students who value its favored activity relatively more highly. In the context of politics, such specialization is not be feasible for national governments, although it may be for localities within a country.

Laffont and Tirole (1993, pp. 225–226) and Tirole (1994, pp. 6–7) develop this idea further. When the output of the agent's effort is an "experience good" whose quality will be revealed only with a delay, then the immediate incentive scheme must be low-powered so as not to destroy the incentive to maintain quality.

Multiprincipal Agencies
Let us turn to the second important feature of government bureaucracies that was pointed out by Wilson, namely, the existence of multiple principals, all of whom have some power to influence the actions of the agency. Their interests in the outputs of the agency are at least partly in conflict, and the agent's actions taken on behalf of different principals are substitutes. How do incentive schemes fare in such a situation? The general conclusion is that the power of incentives in the equilibrium among several such principals is weakened, sometimes dramatically.

Let us begin by asking why common agency is so prevalent. The various principals clearly stand to gain by getting together: the scheme that results from their noncooperative actions remains feasible, so a cooperative scheme cannot do worse and in general will do better. At least two problems may preclude such collusion. First, they may not share the same information, most naturally so in the case of adverse selection. Although this seems to force noncooperative behavior, I will argue later that the compartmentalization of information may actually be beneficial. Second, the multiple principals may find it difficult to agree on the split of the total gain from cooperation, or be unable to make the internal transfers necessary to implement an agreed-upon split. This is particularly important in the political context, where the benefits of the principals are often nonmonetary and are measured in noncomparable, nontransferable units, whereas monetary compensations are often illegal. In the appendix I construct a simple model of common agency with moral hazard to show that the multiplicity of conflicting principals is a powerful additional reason for the incentive schemes to be low-powered. The intuition is that each principal tries to free ride on the incentives provided by the others.

To illustrate the mathematics in simple terms, suppose two principals A and B are trying to influence the agent, who controls two tasks a and b. Principal A is primarily interested in the outcome of a, and principal B in that of b. The amount of effort the agent devotes to the tasks is not observable, but the outcomes are commonly observable to all.

Since the agent's time or effort is scarce, more spent on a will necessarily mean less spent on b and vice versa. Therefore principal A will offer an incentive scheme that responds positively to a-output and negatively to b-output, that is, one that gives the agent a marginal reward for producing more a and a marginal fine or penalty for producing more b. The scheme also has a constant term, or a sure payment, whose level can be adjusted to make sure that the agent is willing to work, that is, to satisfy the agent's participation constraint. Similarly, principal B offers a scheme that rewards the agent for producing more of b and penalizes him for producing more of a.

Now suppose principal A offers a high-powered scheme, that is, one with larger marginal reward for producing an extra unit of a. When the agent responds by making more effort on task a, he gets more money from principal A; but because principal B employs a negative marginal payment for this task, the agent pays more to principal B. In other words, some of A's money simply passes to B via the agent. Recognizing this, principal A will not find it desirable to offer such a high-powered scheme. The leakage of one principal's money to the other is less than one-for-one, so each principal continues to find it desirable to offer some incentives to the agent; but in the final outcome of the whole calculation, that is, the Nash equilibrium of the game of strategy between the principals, the overall power of the incentives received by the agent is quite low.

In the mathematical model, the outcome is very simple: the equilibrium with n principals is exactly as if there is just one hypothetical principal with an objective function that is the sum of all the separate principals' objectives, but the agent's risk aversion is multiplied n-fold. Remember that the more risk averse the agent, the lower the power of the incentive scheme. Thus, the Nash equilibrium incentive scheme with n principals has, roughly speaking, only $(1/n)$-th the power of the second-best scheme that would be offered by one truly unified principal.

The low power of the incentives in turn makes the second result of Holmström and Milgrom even more important. The agent's actions may often be influenced better by prohibiting some activities than by rewarding others with conventional marginal incentives.

One must distinguish different levels of efficiency in the outcomes. The hypothetical ideal with observable efforts and Coasean bargaining between all principals and the agent would be the first-best. Respecting the information asymmetry but allowing all principals to get together and offer a combined incentive scheme would give the second-best. If the principals cannot be so united, their Nash equilibrium is in general a third-best (see Bernheim and Whinston 1986 for the exact relationships among these). In these formal terms, the result above says that the third-best outcome that is achieved has very low-powered incentives.

To do better than the Nash equilibrium, one would have to allow some explicit cooperation among the multiple principals. This may not be feasible in the context of their day-to-day interaction or in the course of what I have called policy acts; but at a prior stage, closer to that of Buchanan's constitution design, we may be able to think of some improvements. One such device would restrict each principal to basing his incentive scheme only on the dimension of the agent's action that is of primary concern to that principal, and would prohibit any attempts to penalize the agent for actions in other dimensions. In the example above, this means that principal A cannot condition his payment to the agent on the output of task b, nor principal B on that of task a. This could be done by preventing each from observing the other's outcome, or forbidding each to act on any such obervation. Now each principal, in order to attempt to induce the agent to put more effort into the task that concerns him (principal), offers a higher-powered incentive scheme. In the resulting equilibrium, the overall incentives scheme is actually higher powered than the one that would be offered by a single unified principal who aggregates the interests of A and B. It is shown in the appendix that in the limiting case where the agent's efforts on behalf of the different principals become perfect substitutes, the equilibrium where the principals are so restricted in their schemes is actually first-best! Thus a constitutional restriction on the actions of principals can improve the power of incentives and can lead to a socially preferable outcome.[8] Of course, as usual, the enforcement of such a constitutional restriction is problematic, given the desire of politically powerful principals in their policy acts to influence every dimension of the agent's activity. Note that even if each of A and B can observe the outputs of both tasks a and b, it may be beneficial to forbid each to take the other into account in setting his own incentive scheme, just as if he could not observe the outcome of the other task. Thus an improvement can result from making the information asymmetry apparently worse. This is like the Lipsey-Lancaster general theory of the second-best: if some market failure precludes the attainment of an ideal first-best, then it is no longer necessarily desirable to let the rest of the markets function without any interference.

Tirole (1994, section 8) suggests that compartmentaliza-tion of responsibilities across different ministries or agen-cies of the government can perform a useful function by placing the onus to create, disclose, and defend each item of information necessary for decisionmaking on the party who is particularly interested in that dimension of policy. This argument for "checks and balances" is similar to that behind the adversarial mode of judicial procedures in com-mon law. This idea is formally modeled and further de-veloped by Dewatripont and Tirole (1995). My argument above is different, but it supports the same conclusion.

A similar phenomenon arises in common agencies with adverse selection; these are studied by Martimort (1992, 1995) and Stole (1990). They assume (as seems appropriate in the context of adverse selection) that each principal can observe only that dimension of the outcome which con-

---

8. Holmström and Milgrom (1990) have a similar result concerning the desirability of restricting side trading among multiple agents of one principal.

cerns his payoffs. Each offers a rent-sharing schedule that makes his payment to the agent a function of that dimension of output. If the two principals collaborate, they will offer a second-best joint schedule that reduces their loss of rent by distorting the agent's actions below their first-best level. When they cannot cooperate, for example, when each cannot observe or act upon the other's outcome, there arises an externality between them. When one principal increases the distortion of his dimension, the agent shifts his action at the margin to the other dimension, to the benefit of the other principal. This is a positive externality, so in the noncooperative equilibrium each principal carries out too little of it. In other words, the noncooperative equilibrium has less distortion than the cooperative one, and so the former is closer to the full-information first-best than the latter. As in the case of moral hazard, the comparmentalization of information increases the power of the incentives toward the first-best.[9]

A very different kind of effect of multiple principals is found in the argument of James Madison in his famous tenth Federalist Paper. He says that when several special interest groups — "factions" in his terminology — are trying to influence the decisions of the government, none of them is likely to prevail over the others, and the result will be the pursuit of general or aggregate national interest. This finds partial support in the formal models of Becker (1983), and most particularly, of Grossman and Helpman (1994). They consider competition among organized special-interest groups to influence tariff policy. They find that if the entire population belongs to one organized group or another, the

---

9. The argument will go the other way if the agent's actions for the two principals are complements; in this case there are further complications including nonuniqueness of equilibrium.

equilibrium policy is one of free trade. But this is a kind of Prisoners' Dilemma: in the process every group gives a contribution in its attempt to influence the decision, so the distribution of the output is not the same as it would be if there were no lobbying at all.

Epstein and O'Halloran (1994) model a common agency with adverse selection in a more directly political setting. Consider two interest groups offering contributions to a legislator in exchange for policies. They find if the strengths of the two groups are very unequal, the resulting policy is the same as it would be if only the stronger group were present, but the rent given to the agent is larger in order to meet the potential competition of the other group. But if the groups attain a minimum strength, which they call a "representation floor," then the agent is no longer captured by one of them, and the resulting policy is efficient. This qualifies Madison's argument from the other side. He feared the emergence of a faction so large that it would constitute a majority and impose its will on others; this result shows that a mere multiplicity of opposing interests is not a guarantee of efficiency unless the smaller factions have a certain minimum size.[10]

Lack of Competition
Tirole (1994, p. 4) offers yet another explanation for the low-powered incentives in policymaking. If there are several agents performing similar tasks and subject to common risks, then each agent's performance can be compared with that of the others to get a better estimate of his effort or

---

10. Cassing and Hillman (1986) have a "catastrophe-theory" model where the political power of a special-interest group collapses suddenly when its size falls below a minimum threshold (see also the exposition in Hillman 1989, pp. 34-5).

skills that were not directly observable. Therefore an incentive scheme based on comparative performance, or "yardstick competition," can be effective and high-powered. In politics and bureaucracy, such competition is often limited or even nonexistent; therefore incentives must have lower power. In some cases, for example provision of some urban services, competition can exist or even be created for the specific purpose of allowing better incentive schemes. We increasingly observe examples of this in garbage collection, mail delivery, and even in policing and prison management; Britain has recently set up an internal market mechanism in its National Health Service. However, the multi-task nature of these activities often precludes the use of such devices to their full extent; there exist other "principals" who are more interested in other dimensions of these agencies such as equity and accountability, and their influence limits the use of competition to promote efficiency (see Wilson 1989, chapter 19).

Lack of Transparency
Spiller (1990) offers a different perspective on the common agency aspect. He considers the Congress and special interests as principals, with the regulators as agents. But these are in a vertical relationship: Congress creates the agency and appoints regulators, who then can convey benefits—economic rents—to the special interests. These interests can reward the regulators by offering them post-government jobs. Congress can use its appointment power to extract these rents in the form of direct or indirect contributions from potential regulators. For example, many regulators are appointed from the ranks of Congressional staff.

This model seems to confirm the worst fears of those who regard government as the pessimum form of economic management; but so long as the agency relationship is necessitated by an underlying information problem (a transaction cost), the system may have found the least-cost way of coping with that problem. If an ethics bill is passed prohibiting a public servant from going on to work or lobby for the industry that he formerly regulated, then the special interests and politicians may find an even costlier way of arranging their relationships. When rents exist, there will be competition for them, and the only question for design of feasible policy is to minimize the costs of that competition.

Transparency is generally regarded as a good thing in policymaking (see Krueger 1990 for a good statement of arguments in its favor). Greater transparency often makes information more accurate and more symmetric; therefore it reduces or even eliminates some transaction costs. To this extent the argument is clearly valid, but the Spiller model suggests that transparency may sometimes make matters worse. Some mechanisms, such as employment links between the public sector and business, may be relatively good ways of coping with transaction costs, but making them more transparent may simply lead to a prohibition on their use, either on moral grounds or because it is a visible symptom of the underlying inefficiency. So long as that basic problem persists, these mechanisms will merely be substituted by other, even less efficient ones.

If it is desirable to preserve some opaqueness for such strategic reasons, the observations of outcomes will not be as informative as they could be, and incentive schemes based on these observables will have to be lower-powered. We saw earlier that diversion of effort into a nonobservable activity lowers the power of incentives based on observable outcomes of other activities; here some other considerations make it desirable to keep some activities unobservable, thus reinforcing that phenomenon.

To sum up, the formal analysis gives some support to Wilson's assertion that government bureaucracies often have low-powered incentives and are subjected to constraints on their behavior. The analysis also casts some new light on the phenomenon. The lack of incentives, and the proliferation of the constraints, are often claimed to be proof of inefficiency of government. Agencies often have to say no. Nothing gets done, or at least requires long delays to ensure that all the constraints have been met. In the model, however, the weak incentives, and the prohibitions or constraints, can emerge as a part of the Nash equilibrium. In other words, they may be a reasonable way for the system to cope with the transaction costs. I would not claim that what one finds in reality is always a constrained optimum, but at least the result suggests that we should not jump to the opposite conclusion either.

2.4   National Differences

Every country has its peculiarities of history, geography, culture, population, language, and many other characteristics that determine the operation and evolution of its politics and institutions. Therefore these factors also affect its ability to cope with the transaction costs that arise in the making of economic policy. Much of the research on what I called transaction-cost politics has been conducted in the United States (although Europe is rapidly gaining ground), and my own thinking and examples also derive from the U.S. experience. Indeed, many of the apparent inefficiencies that I have pointed out and discussed seem peculiar to the U.S. context. Many European or Japanese observers would claim that the issues are handled much better in their countries, and some American commentators, for example Thurow (1992), would be inclined to agree; but before we jump to such a conclusion, we must examine in more detail just how country differences translate into differences in the operation of economic policy.

Wilson (1989, chapter 16) emphasizes two aspects of national differences. The first is between parliamentary systems where the executive has effectively unchallenged authority during the life of a government, and ones with separation of powers and checks and balances as in the United States. He argues that in the latter, every affected interest has many points of entry to be heard and many levels of appeal. The U.S. Constitution in fact guarantees the right to address the government for redress of grievances. The result is that the policy process is continuous and adversarial; "it's never over." In a parliamentary system, Wilson argues, the rivalry is strong and bitter at the level of general elections; but once a stable government has emerged, everyone has to live with it for a number of years. Knowing this, all affected parties use more consensual and flexible approaches.

There are other aspects of parliamentary systems that are less desirable. When a government can use its majority to rule unchallenged during the life of the parliament, there is a risk that it will make major errors that a system more open to procedural delay and more subject to checks and balances might have avoided. The Poll Tax in Britain, now generally recognized as a disastrous political mistake if not a serious ethical error, is an excellent example of such a failure of "elective dictatorship, which gave the government an almost completely free rein" (Butler, Adonis, and Travers, 1994). Further, since each parliament is sovereign, and cannot bind its successor (within the constraints of an overall constitution that is often weak, or in the case of Britain, nonexistent), governments cannot make long-term commitments. Of course, as we saw earlier, in some contexts this may be an advantage.

Wilson's second distinction is cultural. Some countries— he points to Japan and Sweden in particular—have a tradition of deference to authority, including in this term both governance and expertise. Therefore citizens of such countries are less prone to challenging the decisions of bureaucrats or commissions. U.S. citizens have far more individualistic attitudes, and are willing to challenge experts and resist officialdom. This has its advantages, but it does cause much inaction and indecisiveness that foreigners point to as instances of inefficiency.

This issue is analyzed in a theoretical model by Dewatripont and Tirole (1995). Their model introduces a trade-off between two considerations. On the one hand, when information must be created, the adversarial system has the advantage that interested parties have better incentives to do so. On the other hand, if information can be manipulated (concealed or forged), decision making by a nonpartisan authority can be superior.

Levy and Spiller (1994) cast some empirical light on this issue. They examine a sample of countries with very different political systems, focusing on the question of what can ensure a sufficiently stable regulatory system to mitigate fears of arbitrary expropriation and thereby ensure long-term investment. They find that there is not a unique way. Different mixtures of legislative and administrative arrangements can do an effective job, but there must be some effective power that guarantees stability, and an independent and well-regarded judiciary to resolve disputes impartially seems to be an important component of a successful system.

Katzenstein (1985) studied several small European countries with a special focus on their international trade policies. He found that they had evolved a very successful system to cope with the problems and opportunities that the changing world trade environment brings. His name for the system is "democratic corporatism." He defines this (p. 32) as "the voluntary, cooperative regulation of conflicts over economic and social issues through highly structured and interpenetrating political relationships between business, trade unions, and the state." This is conducive to "low-voltage politics," where rival parties have broad areas of agreement about economic policy. The common underlying axioms are: (1) adaptation to changing economic circumstances is inevitable, and (2) the costs of such adaptation should be shared by the whole nation using some form of social insurance. Katzenstein argues that the implementation of these ideas differs widely, with laissez-faire Switzerland at one end and more socialistic Austria at the other, but he identifies many similarities in the overall aim and direction of economic policy in seven countries.

The smallness and homogeneity of these countries plays an important role in the evolution of this system. It enables them to cope with transaction costs in a way that would be difficult for a larger or more heterogeneous country to match. A commitment to social insurance would generate moral hazard — people would take excessive risks in their trading ventures, or otherwise pretend trade-related injury and obtain compensation. In a homogeneous country with a greater sense of identity and common purpose, or a small country where such opportunism can be more quickly observed and exposed, it may be possible to develop long-term reputation or punishment arrangements that limit the costs of the moral hazard. In a large and heterogeneous country like the United States, where the population is mobile, this is far more difficult.

If the United States is particularly subject to transaction costs that are difficult to mitigate, then the rest of the world must face up to some bad news—it is becoming more like the United States in many relevant aspects of politics. Countries are becoming less homogeneous, citizens are becoming less respectful of authority, and procedures are becoming more open, with the result that multiple special interests are able to influence the policy process and its outcomes.

Europe's expansion has made it more heterogeneous. The difficulties of unifying Western and Eastern European countries are particularly dramatic, as Germans know very well from their recent experience. Perhaps in recognition of such difficulties, the emerging European governance system is developing a separation and limitation of powers. This is more like the United States' system and less like those in many individual European countries. International flows of labor, capital, and information have reduced the homogeneity and cultural identity of most European countries, making it harder to sustain the kind of social insurance policies that Katzenstein discusses; indeed, there has been some erosion of these systems even in the small countries he studied, in the decade since his book appeared. Some such evidence of the fraying of the renowned Swedish consensus can be found in Lindbeck et al. (1994, pp. 17–18).

Of course the enlargement of the European union and the greater international mobility of people and ideas have immense benefits in other dimensions, but they do make it harder to achieve the kind of economic insurance that is ideally possible in a small, "family" setting.

Even in Japan, recent developments have reduced the power of, and respect for, authority and bureaucracy. Japan always had its politics in economics, as evidenced by its rice policy, but in most industrial contexts the politics was hidden within the governing party and behind a collusive front of business, bureaucracy, and politicians. I would not presume to forecast how their system of government and administration will change, but it seems a safe guess that Japan will not be able to continue the kind of cohesive and consensual arrangements that it had for the last forty years.

3 Two Case Studies to Illustrate Transaction-Cost Politics

In the preceding chapters, I gathered together several concepts, particularly commitment and agency, under the umbrella of transaction-cost politics, and argued that they help us better understand the process of economic policymaking. I also argued that the process has its dynamics, and it holds surprises for some or all participants. We have to understand the outcomes in the context of history, the constitutional framework, and the inertia that exists in changing institutions and organizations. Many of these ideas are already widely used in particular contexts, most notably regulatory policy (where the transaction-cost perspective is explicitly recognized) and macroeconomic policies (where the explicit connection with transaction-cost economics has not been made). This work is a mixture of theoretical modeling, some supporting empirical evidence, and a little formal hypothesis testing.

In this chapter I will examine two specific problems of economic policy as "case studies" through a transaction-cost politics lens. The cases I have chosen are (1) tax reform in the United States, and (2) the General Agreement on Tariffs and Trade (GATT) and international trade politics. This choice was motivated by the very different contexts and concerns they highlight. The first is about domestic politics within the framework of an overall constitution, and the other is about the design and the constitution of an international organization, and its subsequent operation and evolution.

In each case, I focus on just one key point of political tension, which generates repeated shifts in rules and procedures as the parties to the conflict try to manipulate the system in their own favor. Various transaction costs — particularly information asymmetries, opportunism, and bounded rationality — play important roles in this process. My plan in each case is as follows. I begin by examining the transaction costs that exist in the system, and I identify the major problem or problems they have created for its successful performance. Then I search for the mechanisms that have been developed for coping with these costs.

The format of the case studies combines a narrative of the developments with some informal conceptual discussion of the role played by transaction costs in the story and how the actors in the dramas attempted to cope with these costs. The treatment is brief, as befits the lecture in which the studies were first presented. The approach is neither formal theoretical modeling, nor formal statistical testing, nor detailed historical or institutional analysis. My sole aim is to highlight the transaction-cost aspect of the situations, hoping thereby to convince the reader that these costs are significant in policy issues of major importance, and that the transaction-cost-politics framework is likely to be useful in more detailed studies of these issues. As with the construction of the framework in chapter 2, this work should be regarded as suggestive, not definitive; but at that level I believe it serves well to illuminate the concepts by illustrating them. If these cursory studies stimulate some readers into deeper analyses along these lines, I will think that I have succeeded, regardless of whether the later in-depth studies are theoretical, empirical, or historical, and regardless of whether they support the few tentative conclusions I offer below.

3.1 Tax and Expenditure Reform in the United States

There is a large literature on fiscal policy from the macro-economic angle, focusing on the trade-off between output and inflation, and examining the relation to monetary policy, which implicitly uses several ideas that I have gathered together in the transaction-cost-politics framework. Some of this literature was discussed in Chapter 2. In the United States, however, the most important aspects of tax and expenditure policies, and perhaps the major points at issue when tax reform is discussed, have little to do with macroeconomic stabilization, at least not directly. Instead, what is at stake is the redistribution that is implicit in budgetary decisions—the benefits that various groups and generations in society get from various kinds of government expenditures, and the costs of paying for these benefits in the form of taxes. These microeconomic issues are my focus here.[1]

The key tension in U.S. fiscal politics arises from the fact that different politically important constituencies make simultaneous demands for three mutually incompatible things: larger expenditures, smaller taxes, and balanced budgets. Several important interest groups—farmers,

---

1. I have drawn on many excellent detailed descriptions and analyses, including Wildavsky 1984, Kosters 1992, Cogan, Muris, and Schick (eds.) 1994, Niskanen 1992, and Schultze 1992, and a symposium in the *Journal of Economic Perspectives* in Summer 1987.

senior citizens, cities, declining industries, emerging industries—want the federal government to subsidize or
promote matters of concern to them. All taxpayers want
lower tax burdens. Political pressure is exerted on behalf
of all these groups. Each can claim that its position is
justified by public opinion at large, because opinion polls
show support for one or two or even all three, depending
on just how the questions are framed. Most such polls
find that a vast majority of Americans favors balance in
government budgets, but for a variety of reasons, ranging
from a general belief that "the government should live
within its means" to specific concerns about inflation or
waste. Blinder and Holtz-Eakin (1984) analyzed the findings of some such polls. They found that the single most
important reason for supporting budgetary balance (in the
sense of making the largest incremental contribution to
the probability of favoring balance) was the belief that it
would "reduce wasteful programs," whereas the single
most important reason for opposing such balance was the
belief that it would "reduce necessary programs." The polls
did not go into more specifics, but it seems plausible that
necessary programs are those that favor oneself or one's
close family or associates, whereas wasteful programs are
those that spend resources on other industries, regions, or
ethnic groups.

The range of functions accepted (or even demanded) as
being within the government's role steadily expanded over
the last two centuries, but the basic conflict retained its
nature, at least for the last century.[2]

---

2. Europeans, even the British, seem somewhat better aware of the iron
law of arithmetic that links together expenditures, taxes, and deficits,
and somewhat more willing to pay taxes to get higher benefits (see *The
Economist*, November 19, 1994, pp. 67–68.)

A round in this ongoing debate is being fought in the United States Congress at the time of this writing. Most politicians of both parties have declared deficit reduction to be their paramount concern. However, several previous rounds launched with equal determination did not produce the desired result. A news analysis column by David Rosenbaum in the *New York Times* on 19 May 1995 expressed the situation very well:

"Make no mistake about it, this bill is a historic watershed," said Senator Bob Packwood, Republican of Oregon. "If this bill does not work, or if Congress and the President attempt to frustrate it, we will lose our last significant opportunity to deal with the deficit."

Those sentiments were expressed repeatedly today as the House of Representatives approved a resolution that is supposed to lead to a balanced budget by 2002 and the Senate began debate on a companion measure.

But Senator Packwood's remarks were not made today. They came on the night 10 years ago when Congress approved the Gramm-Rudman-Hollings legislation, which was meant to put the budget into balance by 1991.

The fact is, Congress has been promising a balanced budget ever since 1978, when legislation was adopted stating that beginning in the fiscal year 1981, spending "shall not exceed" receipts.

Politicians and expert commentators assert that "this year feels different"; time will tell.

The issue that underlies all these efforts and their failure is one of intergenerational distribution of economic resources. Kotlikoff (1992) has demonstrated just how large these distributive effects are. He has also pointed out that annual budget deficits or surpluses are not good or valid measures of this underlying reality; a given pattern of real resource distribution across generations can be achieved at the same time as any desired figure for the annual budget deficit by suitably relabeling receipts, payments, and borrowing. However, the budget deficit remains the measure the political debate still focuses on, and it will serve my immediate purpose.

My questions are: Why does the political process so persistently fail to achieve the goal of budgetary balance, declaring it to be so crucial all this time? Can it do better, and if so, how? To think about these questions, we must examine more closely the constitutional rules of fiscal decisions, and the policy acts that are made under these rules.

The U.S. Constitution says very little about tax and expenditure matters. Article 1, section 8—the powers of Congress—stipulates:

The Congress shall have power

1. To lay and collect taxes, duties, imposts and excises, to pay the debts and provide for the common defense and general welfare of the United States; but all duties, imposts and excises shall be uniform throughout the United States.

2. To borrow money on the credit of the United States. . . .

7. To establish post-offices and post-roads.

This is followed by some clauses about raising and maintaining an army, a navy, and militias, and exercising authority over the federal capital and purchased territories. Other sections about establishing a judiciary, and so on, can also be interpreted as mandating expenditures. Article 1, section 9 forbade "capitation, or other direct, tax," but this has been modified by the Sixteenth Amendment. Finally, Article 1, section 7 says that "all bills for raising revenue shall originate in the House of Representatives; but the Senate may propose or concur with amendments as on other bills."

This illustrates perfectly my claim in chapter 1 that constitutions are incomplete contracts. These provisions are very far from establishing a complete contractarian framework of rules that determines all subsequent political acts and leave no degrees of freedom. "General welfare of the United States" can mean anything that the current Congress takes it to mean—anything that the political process of legislation and lobbying will produce and that public opinion will tolerate at the next election. The devil has always been in the details of interpretation and implementation, or in the organizations and procedures of policy acts. These details have changed over time in quite dramatic ways. One procedural feature had a particularly important effect on the outcomes.

For almost the first century of the Congress, the procedure governing expenditures was simple.[3] One committee of the House made all appropriations decisions: the Ways and Means Committee from 1789 to 1865, and the newly formed Appropriations Committee from 1865 to 1877. From then until 1885, several new committees were formed, and spending authority was dispersed among them.

Control of expenditures or deficits had not been a major problem before. The debt accumulated during the Revolutionary War was gradually retired by building budget surpluses; this process was completed by 1835. The debts of the Mexican-American War and even the Civil War were similarly promptly extinguished, but after 1885, expenditures rose rapidly—50 percent by 1893, and 45 percent between 1900 and 1916.

The reason is easy to see in terms of the committee structure. A single committee with expenditure authority has a

---

3. The following account is based on Cogan 1994.

better sense of the opportunity cost of funds, and can better compare the merits of alternative proposals than can multiple committees. Each of several committees has its own spending priorities, which it can better meet by raiding the overall budget. This is "common resource" problem, just like that of several oil companies tapping into a common pool underground. The outcome is a Prisoners' Dilemma.

In a reform enacted in 1919, expenditure decisions were returned to the Appropriations Committee. Fiscal discipline was promptly restored, and the 1920s saw a string of surpluses; but the reform was gradually reversed starting in the 1930s, and by 1974 almost every congressional committee had the power to report expenditure-authorizing legislation to the floor. The common resource problem returned and has grown steadily more severe ever since.

The effect of the initial dispersal of authority was not merely predictable to game theorists and in hindsight; it was predicted by at least some participants and in advance. Congressman Samuel Randall warned in the 1885 debate over the proposal: "If you ... have many committees where there ought to be but one you will enter upon a path of extravagance you cannot foresee the length of or the depth of until we find the Treasury of the country bankrupt." (quoted in Cogan 1994, p. 28). Likewise, Woodrow Wilson said in 1917 in support of the reform: "it will be impossible to deal in any but a very wasteful and extravagant fashion with the enormous appropriations of public moneys ... unless the House will consent to return to its former practice of initiating and preparing all appropriations bills through a single committee." (quoted in Cogan 1994, p. 34).

These episodes seem to suggest the power of procedures to affect budgetary outcomes. They lend credence to the arguments of Wildavksy (1984) and others that the loss of control over the budgetary process has led to the current situation where the budget has ceased to be of value in fiscal forecasting and planning. But the transaction-cost view of the political process points to a need to look deeper and to identify the true underlying political problems, of which the procedures are merely symptoms. Why were the problems allowed to occur, and why did they last so long? The answer must be that the currently dominant forces in the political process wanted just those outcomes and quite deliberately installed or persevered with those procedures.

Although procedures do affect outcomes and have their inertia, ultimately these procedures can be changed, and are changed, in response to the underlying political forces and the outcome of their competition. As in architecture, form follows function. Therefore we must look deeper and examine *why* the committee structures persisted for so long, and why they changed as they did. Two statements in Kosters 1992 express the issue very well. Schick writes: "Americans divide governmental control because they are divided on budget policy" (1992, p. 21), and Penner writes: "[B]udget rules that conflict too severely with political incentives cannot long endure" (1992, p. 19).

In the late 1870s the nation was expanding its geography and its economy; the needs of infrastructure, agricultural support, and so forth, were mounting. If the previous procedures were not conducive to meeting the political pressure for these expenditures, the process would simply change the procedures. Similarly, after World War I, the need to reduce debts was seen to be paramount, and the reform movement acquired more political support. In the 1930s the depression and the New Deal led to increased demand for expenditures. In the 1970s Medicare,

Medicaid, various welfare programs, and many other expenditures grew, and acquired their supporting coalitions. Both of these movements led to a reversion to the dispersal of spending authority. In the 1990s the pressures to control the growth of expenditures and deficits are generating new proposals for reform.

Various procedural reforms that are being suggested now—a two-year instead of a one-year budget cycle, separation of investment from consumption expenditures, a presidential line-item veto, and many others—should be seen in this light. Although their proponents offer them as cures for some pressing problem and as being in the general interest, each will serve one side of the fundamental political conflict better than the other sides. For example, those who prefer larger government expenditures can get around some budgetary restrictions by labeling their preferred expenditures as investment and therefore outside the scope of restrictions on current spending. If the political support for such an interest is genuinely strong enough, a procedural method to implement it will be found and will endure for a while. If procedural reform is enacted without underlying political support, the real forces will find a way round the reform, and the attempt will fail.

We can better understand in this light the two major experiments in expenditure controls that have actually been attempted during the last decade. The Gramm-Rudman-Hollings Act seemed a clear commitment; it mandated equal expenditure cuts from civilian and defense programs to meet well-defined annually declining deficit targets. But it was quickly rendered ineffective by the loopholes it allowed and by the ability of the process to circumvent it by redefining baselines, thereby revising the methods of forecasting or "scoring" (see Muris 1994). The Budget

Enforcement Act of 1990 made an equally clear commitment; it required that any proposed changes in mandatory programs be deficit-neutral: any legislation proposing an increase in expenditures or decrease in revenues must be fully offset by decreases in expenditures on other mandatory programs, or by tax increases, or by sequestration of funds. This has shown some promise, by stopping some proposals from ever being offered for legislation when they would have seemed attractive if separated from their revenue consequences. But it has had some unexpected effects, for example, a small loss of tariff revenue due to the liberalizations agreed upon in GATT's Uruguay Round was threatening to prevent the ratification of that whole agreement by Congress. Also, at least some argue that the act was a mere short-term measure that allowed politicians of both parties to claim that they had solved the problem, and that the structural problems would resurface in the long term. Schick (1992, p. 21) called it the Politicians' Protection Act.

In any normative or policy-design examination of the situation, therefore, we should be aware of these underlying political forces. We should not look for procedures that "cannot endure." The budget process is riddled with these costs. It is extremely complex; therefore it becomes difficult to make and enforce precise distinctions, for example, between consumption and investment. This brings bounded rationality to the fore, makes commitment difficult, and invites opportunistic manipulation by legislators and interest groups. The ultimate effects of most expenditure decisions such as education, health, and even defense are not readily observable, which raises moral hazard problems.

If the current wave of efforts to balance the budget represents sufficiently strong public support, it will yield procedures to implement its objectives, albeit imperfectly and with some delay. However, if the lack of discipline over expenditures is actually due to an underlying political equilibrium where those who benefit from these expenditures are powerful enough to preserve them, then the budgetary problems may get worse until eventually foreign creditors of the U.S. government are able to bring external discipline.[4] Such commitment has been imposed by the International Monetary Fund on many less developed countries, and it may prove equally effective, although equally unpleasant, for the United States.

3.2   The GATT and National Trade Politics

The key political conflict in international trade is a Prisoners' Dilemma for the group countries seeking to agree to a more liberal trading regime. Each country wishes to restrict its trade—sometimes because it wants to exert some national monopoly or monopsony, sometimes because it wants to pursue a strategic industrial policy that is at least in principle in its national interest, sometimes because trade barriers are thought to counter some domestic market failure, but mostly because some interest group powerful in its domestic politics wants protection from foreign competition. If all countries give way to this pressure, all will be losers. Therefore they have an incentive to get together and exchange credible promises of retaining open trade regimes. Of course, each retains an incentive to renege on such an agreement, and then to try and prevent others from doing the same. The story of the GATT is a playing out of

---

4. But Sinn (1988) finds that the path from United States budget deficits to an unsustainable stock of America's foreign debt is a slow one.

these tensions. It is particularly interesting in its demonstration of how quickly a supposedly clean slate gets dirty in the political process.

The end of World War II was as good a time for making a completely new start and laying down new rules and institutions for an international political and economic order as there has ever been. A few major powers had unchallenged ability to impose their will; even after the rift between the Soviet Union and the Western powers, the latter had the freedom for several years to shape all economic arrangements outside the Soviet bloc. They had much experience to draw on; in particular, they could avoid the disastrous mistakes made at Versailles after the end of World War I.

Three international economic institutions emerged from this endeavor—the International Monetary Fund (IMF), the International Bank for Reconstruction and Development (the World Bank), and the General Agreement on Tariffs and Trade (GATT). The last is in some ways the most interesting from the perspective of transaction-cost politics. It was shaped by many unanticipated events, it evolved in ways quite different from those foreseen, and it has a record of important successes as well as failures in its mission. It demonstrates very well the importance of politics and history in shaping economic policy. It carries some important lessons for the attempts to establish the new World Trade Organization and some implications for its future. From the large and complex history of the GATT, I will pick just a few episodes that illustrate the forces and the effects of transaction costs.

There are several excellent histories and analyses of the GATT. From the legal and historical perspectives, Diebold 1952, Dam 1971, Jackson 1990, and Hudec 1990 and 1993 are noteworthy. Staiger (1995) gives a detailed description of several GATT rules and procedures in connection with his survey of the theoretical literature on international trade agreements. Baldwin (1988) also focuses on the economics, while Moser (1990) analyses the political economy of the GATT from a public-choice perspective. Bhagwati (1992), Hathaway (1987), and Snape (1986) consider various aspects of GATT reform. Evans and Walsh 1994 and Collins and Bosworth 1994 are early studies of the structure and the likely economic effects of the new GATT or WTO. Destler 1992 focuses on the politics of U.S. trade policy. I have drawn on all these studies, although I will not always cite them individually.

The GATT was a strange constitution for world trade. It was made by countries with strong perceptions of their economic interests and their domestic political imperatives. In fact, although unbeknown to them, they were behind a veil of ignorance. The economics of world trade shifted faster than GATT did. This produced many surprises, only some of which could be remedied by a change in procedures to bring them into conformity with the changed political realities.

The GATT was not meant to be a permanent organization at all. It was an interim arrangement that was supposed to be replaced by a more powerful body, the International Trade Organization (ITO). This never came into being, because the United States, after playing a leading role in the negotiations that culminated in the ITO charter, failed to ratify it. The reasons were a curious mix of domestic and international politics. The American business community did not support the ITO, some for the usual protectionist reasons, and others for perfectionist ones: they wanted an even more perfect free trade agreement and opposed the exceptions and escape clauses that were placed in the ITO charter at the insistence of one country or another in the negotiations. Other interest groups in the United States, including labor unions, were halfhearted in their support. The Truman administration lacked support in Congress and was unwilling to use up its political capital when more important issues, such as the Marshall Plan and the military buildup for the cold war, demanded more attention. Facing defeat, President Truman withdrew the ITO charter from Congress. In 1950 it was inconceivable for the world to proceed to an international trade agreement without the United States. Therefore the ITO was abandoned, and the GATT was allowed to continue. Diebold (1952) describes and analyzes this episode.

This led to some strange consequences. GATT was not a treaty, although most countries regarded it as such. The results of negotiating rounds had to be given effect in U.S. law by legislation that went the usual route through both Houses, and not by ratification in the Senate, as would be the case for a treaty. Also, the countries in GATT were formally not members, but "contracting parties." A better term used by some economists is "signatories." The usage "members" is common except in GATT's formal documents, however.

Enforcement Mechanisms

Given its temporary purpose, GATT did not set up any effective enforcement procedures. These evolved gradually, under constant resistance from some member countries, and therefore remained weak, but it is not clear whether better mechanisms would have survived the political imperatives brought to the scene by the economically most powerful countries.

The procedure was roughly as follows. If country A violated some GATT agreement, another country B that suffers some economic consequences of this violation could bring a complaint to GATT. A panel was established to examine the complaint, and it made a recommendation. This could include authorization for country B to take some retaliatory measure. The report of the panel was considered by the whole GATT. Its approval could in principle be by majority vote, but since 1959 the custom has been to require unanimity.

The weaknesses of this are numerous and obvious.[5] First, there were long delays in setting up the panels, although panels seemed to report in a reasonable length of time once constituted. Second, when a panel's report was considered by the whole GATT, country A had the de facto ability to veto an adverse ruling. This was like putting the accused on a jury that required unanimity. Third, if a country chose to ignore a ruling, or stalled in its compliance, there was not much that GATT could do. International opprobrium was no match for substantial domestic economic interests. Punitive measures by third countries, which would be much more effective, were explicitly ruled out in the GATT framework.[6] Fourth, if country A restricted some imports from country B in violation of its GATT obligations, then B was typically authorized to restrict some other imports from A. What this did was to hurt some innocent third parties in country A, not those import-competing interests in A who were politically powerful enough to obtain the protection, in violation of A's GATT obligation, in the

---

5. The following account is based on Hudec 1993, Collins and Bosworth 1994 and Evans and Walsh 1994.
6. See Maggi 1993 for a theoretical model that brings out the importance of multilateral punishments in sustaining cooperative trade agreements.

first place. Thus the punishment hit the wrong group in A and was therefore less effective in securing A's compliance (Moser 1990, p. 34). Fifth, the whole process could be bypassed, as the case of voluntary export restraints discussed later reveals. Finally, the whole process was loaded in favor of the larger economic powers and against the smaller ones. The average compliance with panel rulings was quite good (over 80 percent), but the record of the more important larger countries was much worse. (Hudec 1993, p. 362).

In the new WTO, panel reports are to be accepted automatically unless they are appealed by one of the parties and reversed under an established procedure, but the other weaknesses remain. In particular, it is difficult to see how the WTO can prevent voluntary bilateral deals among sovereign countries, particularly if they are the larger economic powers. As we saw earlier in the case of budgetary reform, attempts to strengthen procedures will have little success unless they are backed by the political desire to make them succeed. In world trade such determination is weakened by the pressure of domestic interests.

Since an effective dispute-settlement procedure is an important part of the mechanisms to cope with incomplete contracts, moral hazard, and opportunism, any international trade organization whose powers in this dimension are restricted must remain weak in its ability to deal with these important transaction costs.

Safeguards or Loopholes?

An important principle of the GATT is "tariff binding," whereby a trade-liberalizing tariff reduction, once agreed to, cannot be reversed. Exceptions are allowed, however, to cope with sudden surges in imports that inflict serious harm on domestic import-competing industries, and in some other such instances. These are called "safeguards" or "escape clauses." Nontariff barriers are essentially prohibited in theory, although they are tolerated in practice, and were even officially recognized in a "code of conduct" that was part of the Tokyo Round of GATT negotiations. These may seem blatant licenses to violate or bypass the founding principles or practices of the GATT, but it has been argued that they stem from a recognition of the inherent political weaknesses of the dispute-settlement mechanism, and provide a safety valve that prevents a catastrophic failure. In the analysis of a repeated game of tariff setting that was presented in chapter 2, we saw that there is a limit to the extent of cooperation that can be self-enforcing. A good system will recognize such limits at the outset and not attempt too much liberalization that would be doomed to failure.

When the underlying economic conditions are changing from one play to the next, an additional consideration arises. There may be identifiable occasions when the advantages of cheating are larger. Unless the system allows a limited amount of backsliding on these occasions without triggering collapse of the agreement, it cannot be sustained in equilibrium. In the case of trade liberalization, recessions or import surges in a country create large pressures for protection in its domestic politics. The escape clause allows temporary measures to relieve this pressure and thereby helps hold together the rest of the agreement. Thus, the loopholes may be a reasonable attempt to cope with the transaction costs of the complicated game of domestic and international politics unfolding over time (A theoretical analysis of this comes from Bagwell and Staiger

1990 and was outlined in chapter 2; see also Jackson 1989, pp. 150–152).

Rules versus Outcomes

The GATT and the WTO, like most policy constitutions, lay down rules. So long as these are being followed, the outcomes that result from the mixture of actions and chance are deemed acceptable. The United States has repeatedly expressed its dissatisfaction with the way this operates in the case of Japan. Japanese tariffs, and other formal barriers, are no higher than those of other major industrial countries. But many American companies find it very difficult to penetrate the Japanese market and complain that the rules are not being observed in practice with the proper impartiality. The U.S. government has been sympathetic; the Clinton administration most so. They want to use "objective measures," most commonly shares of United States exports in the Japanese market, as tests of whether Japan is actually complying with the broad rules of nondiscrimination it claims to have.[7]

The idea of using observable indicators when the magnitude that actually concerns us is not observable is, of course, well known in the economics of information. It forms the basis of the theory of incentive schemes to cope with moral hazard. The agent's output is a mixture of effort and chance. It is first-best to reward effort, but if that cannot be observed, using output is the best available substitute. If the Japanese cannot objectively demonstrate their

---

7. There is a lively debate among economists about the facts of the situation (see a summary account in Krugman 1990, pp. 116–119). I do not need to take part or sides in this; my only purpose here is to elucidate some transaction-cost aspects of using rules and outcomes in this context.

compliance with the rules, and if the outcome is objectively measurable, then there is nothing wrong with using that. Of course the optimally designed scheme should recognize that a shortfall in the objective measure could be due to lack of compliance or to chance and should inflict a penalty that attempts to fit the former and not the latter. In other words, the *power* of the incentive scheme, in the sense that was explained in chapter 2, should not be too high.

The more important objection to the United States' position is that our firms' success also depends on their own efforts, which are equally difficult to verify objectively. If the United States wields its political stick on behalf of our firms, they may then relax their own efforts and expect to have export success delivered to them by political means. Coping with one side's moral hazard may aggravate the other side's, and the overall result may or may not be an improvement.[8]

Incidentally, if Japan were to agree to apply "objective measures," say, for autos or auto parts imports from the United States, these would be enforced by a Japanese government agency like the MITI. This would pose an inherent contradiction: it would strengthen the hand of exactly those bureaucrats whom the United States first accuses of controlling trade too much.

Negotiating Rounds for Liberalization

GATT's efforts at trade liberalization were conducted in several major negotiating rounds, culminating in the recent Uruguay Round. The idea was that bringing all relevant parties together to negotiate mutual removal of trade

---

8. See Bhagwati 1992 for a strong, even impassioned, defense of the rules-based system.

barriers in all sectors of the economy would make it easier to find and consummate mutually beneficial accords, by avoiding the need to find several "double coincidences of wants." In one respect the approach was very successful. Tariffs were negotiated downward, until they had effectively ceased to matter for imports into the advanced industrial countries. The most recent cuts in the Uruguay Round, in many cases down to zero, were relatively trivial.

Less-developed countries (LDCs) retained higher tariffs and strict quotas on many manufactures. Formally, this was based on the GATT provision that temporary quotas could be used by countries with balance of payments problems, but the underlying rationale was usually some form of the "infant industry" argument for protection. After some four decades, it was only the poor experience with these measures, not any dynamics of GATT negotiations, that led may LDCs to recent moves toward unilateral trade liberalization (and more general economic liberalization).

More important, the tariff cuts did not eliminate the domestic political pressures for protection in any countries. These found their way into other protectionist measures, arguably with greater economic-efficiency costs than the tariffs they replaced. I shall say more on this soon.

There are some features of the these rounds that deserve special mention, because they bring out various aspects of transaction costs in negotiation. These include two important procedural devices: the "most-favored-nation" (MFN) principle, and "binding." The MFN principle says that any trade concession offered to one country must be automatically and equally available for all. This removes the fear in making preliminary deals that someone else will get a better deal in the future. The requirement of binding prevented countries from raising tariffs that had been lowered as a part of a previous round (except temporarily and under specified circumstances of domestic economic problems). This was to prevent countries jacking up tariffs as negotiating ploys in preparation for a coming round.

One other important point arises in the implementation of a GATT agreement in the member countries' domestic legislation. In parliamentary systems where the executive has de facto unchallenged powers during the lifetime of a government, this is not a problem; but in a system like that in the United States, the independent legislature may take the agreement as a mere starting point of a fresh set of negotiations and attempt to extract further concessions to favor the interests it represents. Foreign countries, fearing this, would not make concessions to the executive in the original negotiations, and the whole process would stall. Therefore it is essential for the legislature to make a credible precommitment. In the United States this has taken the form of the "fast-track" procedure: the legislation is subjected to a straight up-or-down vote, with limited debate and no amendments. Of course the legislature is reluctant to make such a commitment for any extended period, and the necessary frequent renewal becomes an item in the domestic political negotiations. I suspect that the new Europe will have similar separation of powers (in reality if not in theory), and will therefore have to devise a similar commitment mechanism if it is to participate credibly in trade negotiations of the future.

The new WTO is supposed to have a more continuous process of gradual measures of trade liberalization instead of the large fixed rounds of GATT. The merits of the two approaches are debatable, but the rounds have some distinct advantages. First, as we saw earlier, the explicit combination of issues and countries increases the possibility of formation of coalitions with mutually beneficial deals. Second, if industries or sectors are considered in isolation, the particular domestic import-competing interests in a country that is being asked to make concessions in this industry are concentrated with large per capita benefits from continued protection, whereas the beneficiaries of liberalization—consumers of the imported good who benefit from low prices, and all exporters who gain a little as the import-competing sector releases some resources—would be diffuse with small per capita stakes. The rounds bring together all these interests, making it more likely that the overall national interest is shared by most. Finally, the explicit reciprocity highlights the benefits to domestic exporting interests and thereby marshals their support for liberalization (see Moser 1990, p. 22).

Tariffs versus Quantitative Restrictions

The lowering and binding of tariffs caused various domestic import-competing interests to look for other means of protection. The GATT forbids quotas, except (oddly) on grounds of temporary balance-of-payments difficulties. Also, such attempts to circumvent the effects of the agreed-upon tariff cuts could induce the exporting countries to make a complaint to GATT. At the minimum, this would bring the importing country some inconvenience and bad reputation.

The procedural answer was a variety of bilaterally agreed-upon quantitative restrictions—"voluntary" export restraints (VER), "voluntary" restraint agreements (VRA), and orderly marketing arrangements (OMA). The idea was that the importing country would persuade the exporting country to take on the task of restricting trade.

As compensation, and to induce it not to complain to the GATT, it would get to keep the economic rent associated with the restriction. The sums of these rents have been estimated for a number of such restraints, and they are quite substantial.

Rents, at least, are merely transfers between countries. But such restraints also inflict aggregate costs—deadweight losses—since they increase consumer prices above marginal costs, either by simply restricting supply or by facilitating monopoly or oligopoly pricing. For example, where the exporting country had some monopoly power, the reduction in exports might actually improve its terms of trade to an extent that it would actually benefit from the action, which it presumably could not have taken unilaterally for fear of disappointing some of its exporters. In others, where firms in the exporting and importing countries are in an oligopolistic relationship, the restriction can act as a collusion-facilitating device (see Krishna 1989). In all these instances, consumers in the importing country are the losers, but they are not politically organized. There are also large deadweight losses from the monopoly pricing, but these go unrecognized.

Here is an example where the system fails to cope with transaction costs at all efficiently. In part the problem is that tariffs, being an easily visible and controllable instrument of protection, were subjected to liberalization, and the countries had to have recourse to less efficient means of satisfying their domestic political interests. GATT might have done better to be less ambitious and allowed a larger cushion of tariffs to be used in specified circumstances. In other words, something similar to the safety valve of the escape clause would have served the system as a whole better.

In the WTO, such bilateral or small-group voluntary arrangements are formally forbidden, but how that organization is going to enforce this ban on consensual acts between sovereign countries is not clear.

The Multi-Fiber Arrangement

The most complex example of mutually agreed-upon quantitative restrictions is the system of bilateral quotas in textiles and clothing. This is of special interest from the transaction-cost politics perspective. It shows how a constitution has to make exceptions to respond to real forces, and how actions can have long-lasting effects.[9]

The starting point was a "voluntary" agreement to restrict Japanese exports of cotton textiles to the United States. This was concluded in 1957, in response to pressures from United States textile producers, with the aim of giving them some breathing space to adjust and contract. It was supposed to last five years. It led to the growth of imports into the United States from other low-wage Asian countries. Then, under the threat that the United States would impose restrictions unilaterally, these countries were also brought into the agreement. The United States also pressured GATT to sanction this special exception to its MFN principle and its prohibition of quotas. The result was called the Short Term Agreement. Within one year, it became the Long Term Agreement.

This led to a chain of substitution, both in private responses and in policy responses, that is easy to understand in the light of hindsight. Cotton textiles were defined

---

9. The brief history below is based on Yoffie and Gomes-Casseres 1994, chapter 18.

as those with cotton content of 50 percent or more, so exporting countries shifted to blends including synthetic fibers. Asian exporters also expanded in European markets, and these countries wanted to impose their own restrictions. In the meantime Japan's economy had transformed to the point where it became an importer of textiles and clothing, and its producers wanted protection from the low-wage Asian countries' exports. Newer lower-wage exporting countries stepped in to replace the existing exporters subject to the quotas, and they were roped into the agreement whenever they became important enough to be perceived as a threat to the importing countries' domestic producers. Soon the agreement became a multi-country, multi-fiber, multi-garment maze of restrictions.

All the time, the preamble of the agreement paid lip service to the merits of trade: "[T]o promote on a sound basis the development of production and expansion of trade in textile products." But Article 1 of the agreement spoke of "special practical measures ... ensuring the orderly and equitable development of this trade and the avoidance of disruptive effects in individual markets." One does not need to ask what was the true purpose. Every renegotiation of the agreement spoke of allowing trade to expand, but in reality the restrictions were repeatedly tightened. The breathing space for the United States industry has lasted almost forty years. New investment and employment has taken place under the protection of the agreement, and the domestic political forces for protection remain strong.

In the WTO, the quotas of the MFA are to be replaced by "equivalent" tariffs that initially restrict imports to the levels of the current quotas; this process is called "tariffication." The tariffs are then to be gradually phased out over a period of ten years. When we assess the likelihood of this becoming reality, we should remember that the initial textile agreement itself was intended to last for only five years, but has lasted for more than thirty, and has if anything grown more restrictive and all-encompassing over this time. We should not be surprised to see the emergence of some loophole that justifies the perpetuation of the restrictions well into the next century.

Agriculture

Agriculture was treated differently from manufactures in the GATT.[10] Most important, export subsidies (or price supports that had the effect of promoting exports) for manufactures were per se illegal, while those for agricultural products were treated much more leniently. First, they merely had to be reported. Then they were made illegal if they caused the subsidizing country to get "more than an equitable share of world trade"; given the difficulty of defining "equitable," this was a meaningless provision. Similarly, quantitative restrictions could be applied to imports of agricultural products for various reasons including "enforcement of domestic production or marketing restriction measures," to "remove a temporary surplus," and so on. Again, judging these matters was effectively impossible. This special treatment was not the result of demands by the European Community (which did not then exist), nor by Japan (which was not then a member), but by the United States. In fact the special treatment was tailored to the needs of the United States farm programs then in existence. Years later, the provisions were exploited by Europe for its Common Agricultural Policy, and by

---

10. The following brief history is based on Hathaway 1987, pp. 105–106, 108.

Japan for its import bans on rice, beef and so forth. The
United States fought many fruitless battles to extend the
standard GATT rules to agriculture.[11]

The new GATT, or WTO, seeks only a partial reform.
With a long transition period, export subsidies are to be
cut by an average of 36 percent, and price supports by
20 percent. Nontariff barriers are to be converted to their
equivalent tariffs. In some cases such tariffs are very high,
for example, the tariff equivalent to Japan's import ban has
been variously estimated at somewhere between 450 percent and 700 percent. Over a longer period, it is hoped that
these tariffs will be negotiated downward.

This is probably as much as could be hoped; Hathaway
(1987, pp. 142, 144–145) counseled a similar compromise.
But what are the prospects of even this much being realized? Again, I believe that the countries' commitments reflected in these agreements are not by themselves credible.
If their internal political forces a year later call for a continuation of the existing supports or protection, a way will be
found to continue them. In the case of a powerful bloc like
Europe or a powerful country like Japan, the WTO will be
unable to prevent this, and will sanction a special arrangement just like the MFA. The hope must be that during the
intervening period, the power of the agricultural groups
in these countries will wane. Political economy offers some
theoretical support to the idea that the power of special interests collapses when they get too small (see Cassing and

---

11. A similar "biter bit" story comes from the auto industry. In the 1950s
Japan and Italy concluded a bilateral agreement to restrict imports of autos
from each other to a very small number. This move was initiated by Japan,
which feared that its industry would not be able to compete with Italian
imports. Two decades later, this agreement became the basis for serious
market share restrictions on Japan's auto exports to all of the European
Community.

Hillman 1986, Hillman 1989, pp. 34–35, and Epstein and O'Halloran 1994). But food self-sufficiency has a powerful emotional or nationalistic ring, and agriculture has cultural or sentimental appeal in many countries, especially Japan and France. Therefore, the outcome is difficult to predict.

Since GATT mixes elements of domestic and international politics, it is not surprising that its mechanisms to cope with transaction costs work less well than those in domestic politics alone. Shortfalls from an ideal standard of efficiency are easy to spot, but finding feasible changes — remediability — is much harder. The only general finding seems to be the merit of accepting the second- or third-best, for example, allowing some limited and temporary escape clauses even when they depart from the ideal, so long as they are an important requirement to help preserve the larger system over the longer haul.

4   Some Reflections and Suggestions

In the preceding two chapters I have developed and illustrated some themes of transaction-cost politics. What general lessons can we learn from this approach? How does it affect our understanding of the process of policymaking? And what principles should guide economists when they analyze or recommend alternative policies? These questions, already basic, become even more important in view of the observation that the politics of economic policy everywhere is becoming more like that in the United States, and transaction costs of various kinds are looming larger in all policy contexts. Unfortunately, the same analysis also points to the difficulty of giving any general answer to such a question. First, politics intervenes even at the level of spotting and using the degrees of freedom. Normative intervention, and the economist's role in it, involve quite subtle informative and manipulative tactics. Second, transaction costs are only a subset of all kinds of costs. Strategies that would reduce transaction costs, most notably commitments, require some tradeoffs in the form of loss of potentially valuable flexibility. Third, the nature and severity of transaction costs, as well as the available means for mitigating them, differ from one country to another and from one time to another. Therefore any general assertions concerning policy must be few, broad, and tentative.

However, many of these balancing considerations are well understood, whereas the recognition of the role of transaction costs in the policy process is relatively new. Therefore it is worth pointing out and stressing the implications of the transaction-cost politics approach for some desiderata of policy design, and for the role of economists in this process. I will therefore now temper a lot of hesitation with a little pretense of confidence and offer some tentative speculations and suggestions.

4.1 Some Lessons for the Policy Process

Let me begin by summarizing some themes that appeared frequently in the previous chapters. The first theme concerns the relationship between policy rules and policy acts. We have seen that every occasion of policymaking occupies a point somewhere along the continuum between the two pure or polar conceptual categories identified by Buchanan: constitution-making or rule-setting on the one hand, and individual policy acts on the other. If the instance under discussion is closer to the constitution extreme, more degrees of freedom are available. However, the decisions being made have longer-lasting effects and must cover a broader range of issues and circumstances; therefore the choices must strike more compromises between different considerations and give weight to adaptability. If the instance is closer to the policy-act end, the particular circumstances of individuals and groups get greater play, but there are fewer degrees of freedom left for normative considerations. Every occasion involves some element of political conflict, some constraints inherited from history, and some ability to create new facts and consequences of varying degrees of durability.

The second theme concerns complexity and uncertainty. Constitutional rules can only cover a subset of the vast range of circumstances that can be anticipated, and they fail to anticipate an even greater range of possibilities. When circumstances arise for which no explicit provisions have been made, some general dispute-resolution mechanisms or residual rights of control are invoked. These may be inappropriate to the situation, but inertia or hysteresis keeps them in force until the shift is large enough to require a major change in the rules. The evolution of the policymaking process is a story of such surprises, inertia, and changes of policy regime.

The next theme is the large one of information asymmetries. Moral hazard and adverse selection constrain feasible policies to a subset that satisfies the conditions of compatibility with the information and incentives of the participants. Opportunism and the difficulties of making credible commitments can restrict policies by the requirements of time-consistency. In all these cases, there exist various devices to mitigate the problems; but none of them work perfectly, and the ideal of a first-best that would result if the information asymmetries did not exist is almost never attainable. Various information problems can even interact; a scheme that mitigates moral hazard may worsen adverse selection, or vice versa.

The policy process is a complex game of strategy with many players. The incentive schemes to cope with information asymmetries are often limited even more severely by the existence of multiple principals who simultaneously and separately attempt to influence the actions of the proximate decisionmaker. When different actions of this agent benefit the principals differently, and are substitutes in the way they affect the agent, the Nash equilibrium of the game between the principals ends up with very weak incentives. A better outcome cannot be attained unless the principals can act in unison, or a constitutional rule can restrict their incentive schemes in suitable ways.

The last two paragraphs point to an important theme concerning the normative evaluation of different policies, judgments that existing policies are inefficient, and recommendations of better alternatives. All such arguments should recognize the full set of constraints on policymaking: the historically determined rules that cannot be changed within the current context, the information asymmetries, the independent actions available to various political principals, and so on. A policy should not be condemned as inefficient unless a superior alternative that respects all these constraints can be demonstrated; this is Williamson's criterion of remediability.

Many apparently inefficient outcomes can in fact be understood as consequences of constraints imposed by various transaction costs, or as creditable attempts to cope with them. For example, the weakness of incentives in bureaucracies can be seen as a consequence of their being open to influence of multiple principals, and the failure of international trade agreements to achieve complete free trade can be seen as a condition of their having to be self-enforcing against temptations of individual countries to sneak some protectionist actions.

This is not a Panglossian assertion that "everything is for the best in this, the best of all possible worlds"; the best of all possible worlds would not be beset by transaction costs. Rather, it is a reminder of how much policy freedom is constrained by transaction costs. It is saying, "This world is far from being ideal; but a would-be policy innovator would do well to think whether the existing setup is making the best of, or at least coping quite well with, the world's imperfections." It is closer to the old saying about "not letting the best be the enemy of the good." If the best outcome we would like to see violates the incentive constraints, then an attempt to implement it may in fact end up producing something even worse than the current situation, unsatisfactory though that may be.

However, an opposing argument comes from longer-term considerations. Some constraints on policy can be removed or relaxed in course of time. Some exist to cover contingencies that are no longer relevant or are mere historical accidents; these can in principle be removed when an opportunity for a reform of rules arises. Some information asymmetries can be reduced by developing better monitoring technologies or different institutions, organizations, or cultures. Therefore calculations of the economic benefit that can in principle be achieved by removing or reducing constraints have value as guides to long-run action.

In the light of these themes, we can now state some tentative lessons, both for observers of the policy process and for active participants in this process.

Begin with the observers, typically economists. When these observers judge the performance of a policymaking system, they should admit the legitimacy of noneconomic goals and ask if a feature of the outcome that appears prima facie inefficient is in fact a reasonable way of striking a balance between the various interests, or multiple principals, given the transaction constraints.

When the observers make pronouncements as judges of outcomes or systems, they should not try to impose, and perhaps should not even think in terms of, too stringent or idealistic standards of some kind of "first-best" that ignore transaction costs.

As advocates of longer-term improvements, economists can usefully calculate and publicize the economic loss that results from transaction-cost constraints and therefore the value of removing or reducing these constraints. But the nature of the calculation and its implications should be clear: this activity should not be misinterpreted as advocating an immediate shift of policies without first taking measures to relax the constraints.

Next, consider some lessons for actual policymakers. Where degrees of freedom are available for normative use, policymakers should try to put in place, and facilitate the operation of, various "coping mechanisms." They should work to reduce informational asymmetries and improve mechanisms that can control opportunism. Conversely, they should try to avoid policies that create new transaction costs or increase existing ones. Policies like import quotas and price controls, which create artificial rent and then lead to political games to capture and perpetuate these rents, are particularly pernicious in this regard. Of course, many actors in the political process are trying to achieve exactly the opposite, namely, to create rents that they can then appropriate for their private ends regardless of the social costs. The economist's informative and persuasive role is very important in countering these forces.

Where specific investments—economic sunk costs or political commitments—are needed, policy should try to match the two sides' burdens and opportunities, and ensure sufficient longevity of their interaction, to enable them to avoid exploitation using mutual "hostage" or "reputation" mechanisms.

Transparency is desirable when it reduces information asymmetries and removes some transaction costs, but there may be some merit to opaqueness if it conceals relatively efficient ways of coping with transaction costs, while exposing these to public scrutiny and criticism would merely lead to the use of other substitutes that are worse and more deeply hidden.

Repeated attempts to pursue chimeric goals like completely free international trade, or constantly balanced budgets, seem like Dr. Johnson's characterization of remarriage, "a triumph of hope over experience." By contrast, Krugman's "age of diminished expectations" may be merely an age of realism, or a triumph of experience over hope.

4.2 The Role of the Economist

Economists are observers of the political process of economic policymaking. When they study the operation of the process and the consequences of altering any policies or rules, and publicize their findings, they also become participants in the process. Their calculations or forecasts of the economic consequences of various policy acts or rules become one component of the process, but we should not expect it to be a dominant or determining factor.

This raises a crucial question. When we consider the economic impacts of various policy proposals and offer them for public debate, to what extent should we subsume the political process in our calculations? Should we present the economic results our policy proposals would have if they were implemented in a nonpolitical environment, or should we "filter" them through the political process as we understand it? Should economists try to maintain some ideal of "scientific objectivity," or should they accept a more explicitly political role? Strong arguments exist on both sides of the issue.

A former White House political adviser, Stuart Eizenstat, has argued that "economists must ... have the courage to make recommendations based on sound economic judgements, leaving it to others to insert political considerations" (Eizenstat 1992, p. 71). This argument appears to assume that economic and political aspects are additively separable in their effects—that one can analyze each separately and then find the total effect by adding together the two calculations. But that is not in general true. The effects of one interact with the other, and one aspect cannot be inserted after the other to get a complete and accurate picture. Either the economist must include politics in the analysis from the outset, or the political analyst must redo the economics. If neither party is qualified to assess the pertinent aspects of the other's domain of specialization, the two should collaborate from the outset. A purely economic calculation followed by a purely political one does not appear to be a useful compromise.

Some proponents of the scientific approach argue that purely technical or economic calculations of the effects policies would have if they were implemented as recommended, that is, without having to pass through the further stage of alteration or modification for political ends, serve as ideal or benchmark calculations that can inform and influence the political process in desirable directions. Recall the lesson from Herbert Stein cited at the beginning of this book: politicians know even less than economists do about the economy. Some of them are aware of this, and are willing to listen. As Lee Hamilton, who was vice-chairman of the Joint Economic Committee of the United States Congress, put it, "one of the most useful roles an economist can perform is to remind policy-makers that the economy is complex, ... that choices must be made among competing objectives. We politicians don't always want to hear these things, but it is important that we do" (Hamilton 1992, p. 61). In this view, were it not for the standard of purity held up by economists, the political outcome would be even worse.

Evidence on this point is mixed. Many economists have calculated and widely publicized the high costs of import protection (see the collection and synthesis of such studies for the United States in Hufbauer, Berliner, and Elliott 1986, and Hufbauer and Elliott 1994). The inefficient policies persist, and their total cost to the United States economy runs into tens of billions of dollars every year. This seems to support the pessimistic view of the impact of economics on politics. However, in the United States at least, the economists' consistent voice against protection has had an important general and lasting effect. A presumption in favor of free trade prevails; on any specific occasion and with regard to any particular industry, the burden of proof is on those who want protection. Without this requirement, many more industries might have obtained similar protection, and the cost to the economy might have been multiplied manyfold. This seems to support Hamilton's view quoted above.

However, in many of these arguments it is not even clear just what should be regarded as "scientific" economic analysis or research. Should this mean studies of the workings of markets and other voluntary arrangements of activity that is "purely economic"? That would be taking too narrow a view of economic activity. Firms and groups of individuals pursue their economic interests through the political process as much as they do using actions that are more conventionally classified as economic. Some have found the political activity of lobbying for subsidies or protection a better way to profitability than costly economic activities like research and development, or better marketing. An objective scientist should surely insist on including the political process in a positive analysis of the economy. The importance of the political dimension may differ in different contexts, and some narrowly delimited problems may be studied quite effectively without inclusion of political considerations, but the term "scientific" surely should not be construed so narrowly as to exclude the positive study of political economy.

A more legitimate boundary can be drawn when one considers economists' *actions* in the policy process. The difference is between a purely informative role and a directly participatory one. Consider the case of trade policy. In the political arena, this is the outcome of the confrontation of different interests. Economists can participate in this game in either of two ways. First, they can quantify the gains and losses that are at stake, and thus give better information to the principals in the political negotiation as to exactly what their interests are, where concessions can be sought or given, and where the size of the pie can be expanded by changing the constraints. Second, they can directly try to affect the rules of the bargaining game, using strategic moves of their own. Thus they can stake out a pure position in favor of free trade, based on arguments of the total national interest, and try to align public opinion on their side. What economists' arguments about the economic merits of free trade and the costs of protection seem to have accomplished is to frame the rules of the game in such a way that the position they favor has acquired the advantage of the status quo, and the burden of proof lies on any special interest group that wants to depart from this norm. To do so the special interests must fight harder, and they win less often or in less extreme ways, than would be the case if intervention were the presumptive status quo and the case for free trade had to be argued afresh every time.

In practice, economists have played both roles, informative and directly participatory, but with somewhat different emphasis at different points of the policy process. The active participation role becomes more important when more basic or longer lasting decisions are being made, closer to the constitution-making end of the spectrum. These opportunities generally arise at times of "breaks" in the system; when major flaws in the previous arrangements are apparent, there is greater willingness to work toward a better set of rules. The creation of rules and organizations for international trade and monetary arrangements after World War II is perhaps the most prominent example of such a window of opportunity for economists to participate in the policy process. Other examples include the New Deal, and more recently, reform of the U.S. health care system. Even on these occasions, however, economists are far from unanimous as to the right course of action, their participation is not necessarily the decisive or even the most important component of the political process, and the outcomes often contain surprises for all the participants.

The information role of the economist is an ongoing one, affecting policy acts as well as more major reforms of rules and institutions. Here the economic analysis can be relatively straightforward and "technical," although there is much room for differences of judgment and therefore differences in forecasts of what will happen if particular policies are followed. The principals in the political process come armed with the forecasts that favor their position. In the final outcome, the influence of the economists may be quite small. The policies that emerge are generally not in the pristine form that was assumed by the economists who made the calculation, and are further modified in their actual implementation. Therefore the purely informational or benchmark nature of the economists' technical calculations must be admitted and recognized explicitly. Such analyses should not pretend to be forecasts of the actual effects the policies would have in the actual form in which they are likely to emerge from the political process.

When and in what role are economists most effective? In the quote at the beginning of the first chapter, Alan Blinder asserted a paradox: economists are most effective when they are least agreed among themselves, and least effective when they are most agreed. There are examples that support this. Most economists agree on the merits of more liberal trade policies and on the defects of urban rent controls, but the special interests that favor trade protection and rent controls often win the political game. Conversely, no issue divides economists more bitterly than that of the correct underlying model of the macroeconomy. At one time or another, one side seemed to have won the battle and had great effect on policy — the Keynesians in the mid- and late 1960s, and the supply-siders in the 1980s. However, Blinder's paradox seems to be overstated. Economists' arguments and participation have fundamentally affected the trade policy process — the burden of proof still lies on those favoring protection, and their task is made harder. As for the triumph of one side or the other among macro-economists, closer inspection shows that in each case the reason why the actual policies were followed was purely political, and the economists' arguments were merely useful as convenient justifications (see Stein 1984, pp. 113–122 and Blinder 1987, pp. 90–98).

Ultimately, the normative question of what role economists *should* play has as little relevance as does purely normative analysis of economic policy itself. In reality, economists are going to do both kinds of analysis, narrowly economic and broadly political; they are going to play both kinds of roles, detached and partisan, informative and participatory; and they are going to experience a mixture of successes and failures. I have argued that the policy process should be thought of as an evolving, dynamic game; perhaps the economists' role in this process should be viewed in a very similar manner.

4.3 Concluding Comments

Ever since I started planning and thinking about these lectures, I knew that the task I undertook was far bigger than what could be accomplished in the time available for me either to prepare or to deliver them. Things quickly got worse—the subject kept growing as I kept chasing it. In the end I realized that whatever I produced would be only the beginning of a research program, not the finished product of one. But that is perhaps natural for a perspective that emphasizes the complex dynamics and uncertainty of the political process. Why should the research process be any different?

I hope that an incomplete research program is in some ways more satisfactory for the listeners and the readers. I hope some of them will find this an exciting topic and an attractive approach to it, and will join the effort to take it further than I have done here.

Perhaps even more important, I hope this will prove to be a small but useful input in what Ordeshook (1990) called "the emergence of the new discipline of political economy." Social sciences that were once united have split apart in the last century or so. Economics took a more technical route, while politics, sociology, and jurisprudence took more descriptive, historical, or philosophical approaches. Recent developments in all these disciplines are bringing them back closer together. Economists have begun to pay more attention to history and institutions, while political scientists, sociologists, and even legal scholars have become more willing to accept formal mathematical modeling and statistical testing of their theories. This may one day lead to a reunification—an "Einheit der Staatswissenschaften" (unity of the sciences of the state)—which many thinkers in all these fields would like to see. Best of all, this promises to be a genuine merger or a partnership of equals, combining the strengths and the special contributions of all the component disciplines, and not a takeover of one discipline by another, of the kind that economists sometimes threaten other social sciences with. Let us hope that such a partnership proceeds more smoothly than is sometimes the case with mergers of firms, or with economic or political unions of countries!

Appendix:
Multiprincipal,
Multitask Agencies

Here I shall develop a simple formal model of an agency with multiple tasks and multiple principals. In the text I argued that the latter, or *common agency*, aspect is in some ways the quintessential feature of a process of *political* management of an economic activity. I also claimed that the result is low-powered incentives, and that the power of incentives can be restored if a constitutional rule can restrict each principal to base his incentives only on the dimension of the agency's tasks that is of direct concern to that principal. The purpose of the model is to demonstrate these propositions.

The analysis combines the multitask agency models of of Holmström and Milgrom (1990, 1991), and the common agency model of Bernheim and Whinston (1986). After the work was completed, I discovered an older unpublished paper, Holmström and Milgrom 1988, which includes a two-dimensional version of my model but focuses on a different set of issues.

The Model

The agent controls an m-dimensional vector t, to be interpreted as the effort. This yields an m-dimensional output vector x, which is most simply modelled as effort plus an error term

$$x = t + \epsilon, \tag{1}$$

where the random vector ϵ is normally distributed with mean 0 and diagonal variance matrix Ω. This setup can easily be generalized, allowing different dimensions for effort and output with a rectangular matrix linking the two, and error covariances (nondiagonal Ω), but these are not necessary for my present purpose.

There are n principals, who stand to benefit from the output x. It is important here that all the principals observe the same outcome vector x. This seems reasonable in many public policy contexts where there is a great deal of stress on openness of procedures and outcomes, but we will find that such openness is not without its cost.

I assume that the principals are all risk-neutral; so their benefit functions are linear. (Risk-aversion can be introduced at the cost of some notational complexity, but makes no difference for my purpose.) Write $b^{j'}x$ for the benefit function of the j-th principal; the superscript j identifies the principal, and the prime denotes the transpose of the vector. Let b be the sum of the b^j, so the aggregate benefit of all the principals is $b'x$.

A special case that I will take up later is one where the number of principals n equals the number of tasks m, and each principal benefits from only one dimension of the tasks, so that the j-th component of b^j is positive and all other components are zero. More generally, any differences among the b^j correspond to conflicts of interest among the principals and lead to similar results.

It is even possible for some components of some of the vectors b^j to be negative, that is, some principals may be harmed by some dimensions of the output, but I will assume that output is beneficial for the group of principals as a whole, that is, $b \gg 0$.

The agent's utility function has constant risk-aversion:

$$u(w) = -\exp(-rw) \tag{2}$$

where w equals money income minus a quadratic cost of effort, $\frac{1}{2} t' C t$. The matrix C is assumed to be positive definite, and with positive cross-partials (supermodular). Thus, the marginal cost of making one type of effort increases with the level of any type of effort. Therefore, an inducement to increase one type of effort causes substitution away from other types. This creates for each principal an interest in all dimensions of the effort of the agent, even if he has no direct interest in (benefit from) the outcome of those dimensions.

Let Γ denote the matrix inverse of C. It is positive definite, so its diagonal terms are positive. If $m = 2$, it is easy to verify that the off-diagonal terms in Γ are negative. If $m > 2$, some off-diagonal terms may be positive, but the general tendency is for them to be negative. This is exactly like the well-known relationship in consumer-choice theory between complements and substitutes in the quantity (Allen) sense and the price (Hicks) sense. When discussing the results below, I will proceed treating the off-diagonal terms in Γ as negative, leaving it to the reader to fill in the qualifying remarks.

An extreme case is one where the matrix C has the same scalar entry k in all positions, so efforts are perfect substitutes and

$$t' C t = k \left[\sum_{j=1}^{m} t_j \right]^2 .$$

The analysis below does not formally apply in this case because the matrix C is singular whereas we need C^{-1}, but we can consider the case as a limit.

First-Best with Observable Effort

If effort can be monitored directly, the principals and the agent can write a contract contingent on the agent's making a stipulated effort t in return for a payment z. The expected return to the principals will be

$$E[b'(t + \epsilon)] - z = b't - z,$$

and the agent's utility will be

$$-\exp\{-r(z - \tfrac{1}{2}t'Ct)\}.$$

Then, the agent maximizes $z - \tfrac{1}{2}t'Ct$, which is in units of income, and can therefore be thought of as an income-equivalent of the agent's utility.

The z merely acts to transfer income between the parties, for example to make sure that the agent gets enough utility to make it worth his while to participate in this activity. The interests of all parties are best served by choosing t to maximize the sum of the principals' benefit and the agent's equivalent income, or the *total surplus*

$$b't - \tfrac{1}{2}t'Ct.$$

The first-order condition for the maximization is

$$b = Ct,$$

yielding

$$t = \Gamma b. \tag{3}$$

Second-Best with United Principals

Now suppose the effort cannot be observed, and incentive schemes for the agent must be conditioned on the observable outcome x. I will restrict attention to a linear reward scheme. Holmström and Milgrom (1987) have shown that this is without loss of generality if the quadratic payoffs arise in a reduced form of a continuous-time dynamic model where the error ϵ cumulates as a Brownian motion. Even otherwise, linear schemes can be justified as approximations or on grounds of simplicity; they go naturally with quadratic payoffs; and are similarly used in Holmström and Milgrom 1988, 1990, and 1991 without formally specifying an underlying continuous-time dynamic model. I shall proceed on a similar basis.

We continue to suppose that all the principals act together as a benevolent dictator. Of course they remain constrained by the unobservability of effort. Suppose they contract to pay the agent $\alpha' x + \beta$ when the outcome is x. The agent's expected utility from making effort t is

$$-\exp\{-r(\alpha'x + \beta - \tfrac{1}{2} t'Ct)\}$$

$$= -\exp\{-r\,\alpha't + \tfrac{1}{2} r^2\alpha'\Omega\alpha - r\beta + \tfrac{1}{2} r\,t'Ct\},$$

using the standard formula for the expectation of the exponential (moment generating function) of a normally distributed variable, for example, Billingsley 1986, p. 286. This can be written as $\exp(-ry)$ where

$$y = \alpha't + \beta - \tfrac{1}{2} r\,\alpha'\Omega\alpha - \tfrac{1}{2} t'C\,t.$$

This much sure income will give the agent the same utility as the actual uncertain prospect, and it can therefore be thought of as the agent's *certainty-equivalent income*. The agent's decision then consists of maximizing this certainty-equivalent income. The first-order condition for that is

$$\alpha - C\,t = 0,$$

or

$$t = \Gamma\alpha. \tag{4}$$

Remember that diagonal terms in Γ are positive, while its off-diagonal terms are generally negative. Therefore an increase in one component of α will increase that component of the agent's effort and generally decrease the other components.

Substituting for the agent's effort, his certainty-equivalent income becomes

$$y = \alpha'\,\Gamma\,\alpha + \beta - \tfrac{1}{2}\,\alpha'\,\Gamma\,\alpha - \tfrac{1}{2}\,r\,\alpha'\,\Omega\,\alpha$$

$$= \tfrac{1}{2}\,\alpha'\,\Gamma\,\alpha - \tfrac{1}{2}\,r\,\alpha'\,\Omega\,\alpha + \beta. \tag{5}$$

The unified principals' expected income is

$$E[b'\,x - \alpha'\,x - \beta] = (b - \alpha)'\,t - \beta$$

$$= (b - \alpha)'\,\Gamma\,\alpha - \beta. \tag{6}$$

The principals' optimal policy is to choose α to maximize the sum of (5) and (6), or the joint surplus

$$(b - \alpha)'\,\Gamma\,\alpha + \tfrac{1}{2}\,\alpha'\,\Gamma\,\alpha - \tfrac{1}{2}\,r\,\alpha'\,\Omega\,\alpha = b'\,\Gamma\,\alpha - \tfrac{1}{2}\,\alpha'\,(\Gamma + r\,\Omega)\,\alpha,$$

and then choose β to transfer enough to the agent to meet his participation constraint. The first-order condition for α is

$$\Gamma\,b - (\Gamma + r\,\Omega)\,\alpha = 0,$$

or, multiplying by C,

$$b = (I + r\,C\,\Omega)\,\alpha, \tag{7}$$

where I is the m-dimensional identity matrix. We can compare this outcome with the first-best above. If $r = 0$, (7) becomes $b = \alpha$, and then (4) yields $t = \Gamma b$, the same as in the first-best. Now let $r > 0$, and recall that C has all positive elements because it is positive-definite and supermodular, and that Ω has positive entries on its diagonal and zeros elsewhere. Further, so long as negative values of t are economically irrelevant, we can set $\alpha > 0$. Combining all this information, we have

$$b - \alpha = r\,C\,\Omega\,\alpha > 0,$$

or $b > \alpha$. Thus the incentive scheme based only on observables gives the agent less than the marginal contribution of his effort in each dimension. This in turn leads to less effort, and a smaller total surplus. The outcome is a second-best. This reflects the usual trade-off between efficiency and risk-sharing, and it was mentioned in chapter 2 as a transaction cost arising from moral hazard.

Third-Best with Separate Principals

Here the principals do not act cooperatively. Each chooses an incentive scheme, the agent responds to the whole set of incentives he faces, and we look for the Nash equilibrium of the principals' choices. Effort remains unobservable, so each principal's scheme must be based on the observable outcome x. Once again I restrict attention to linear schemes. This was discussed in the case of one principal above; a new point arises for common agency. Given the Holmström–Milgrom (1987) conditions, any one principal can achieve his best response using a linear scheme without loss of generality if all the other principals are also using linear schemes. Thus there is an equilibrium in which linear strategies are used. However, there may be other equilibria involving more complex schemes, which I do not consider. Holmström and Milgrom do likewise in their two-dimensional multiprincipal model (1988).

Denote principal j's linear schemes by $\alpha^{j'} x + \beta^j$, and let $\alpha' x + \beta$ be the aggregate of these scheme. The agent's choice is as in the second-best, namely, $t = \Gamma \alpha$, and his certainty-equivalent income is again given by (5). But now we must examine separately the relationship between each principal and the agent. For this, we have to ask what *difference* it makes when the agent deals with the j-th principal.

For this, let us define the parameters of the incentives schemes aggregated over all the agents *except j*,

$$A^j = \sum_{k \neq j} \alpha^k, \qquad B^j = \sum_{k \neq j} \beta^k .$$

If principal j did not exist, the agent would choose $t = \Gamma A^j$. His resulting certainty-equivalent income can be calculated as in (5), and it equals

$$\tfrac{1}{2} A^{j'} (\Gamma - r \Omega) A^j + B^j$$

Including principal j, the agent's certainty-equivalent income is given by (5). Recognizing that

$$\alpha = A^j + \alpha^j , \qquad \beta = B^j + \beta^j ,$$

we can write this as

$$\tfrac{1}{2} (A^j + \alpha^j)' (\Gamma - r \Omega) (A^j + \alpha^j) + B^j + \beta^j .$$

Therefore the *addition* to the agent's surplus that arises from his relationship with principal j is

$$A^{j'} (\Gamma - r \, \Omega) \, \alpha^j + \tfrac{1}{2} \, \alpha^{j'} (\Gamma - r \, \Omega) \, \alpha^j + \beta^j \, .$$

Principal j's expected surplus is

$$b^{j'} t - \alpha^{j'} t - \beta^j = (b^j - \alpha^j)' \, \Gamma \, (A^j + \alpha^j) - \beta^j \, .$$

His surplus in the absence of the relationship with the agent would have been $b^{j'} \Gamma A^j$, so the difference,

$$b^{j'} \Gamma \, \alpha^j - \alpha^{j'} \Gamma \, \alpha^j - A^{j'} \Gamma \, \alpha^j - \beta^j \, ,$$

is attributable to the relationship.

Once again, the β^j merely serves to transfer the surplus between the parties, and principal j will optimally choose α^j to maximize the total bilateral surplus

$$b^{j'} \Gamma \, \alpha^j - r \, A^{j'} \Omega \, \alpha^j - \tfrac{1}{2} \, \alpha^{j'} (\Gamma + r \, \Omega) \, \alpha^j \, . \tag{8}$$

Principal j, who is acting noncooperatively with respect to all the other principals, will make this choice of α^j treating A^j as given. The first-order condition is

$$\Gamma \, b^j - r \, \Omega \, A^j - (\Gamma + r \, \Omega) \, \alpha^j = 0 \, ,$$

or, multiplying by C,

$$b^j = (I + r \, C \, \Omega) \, \alpha^j + r \, C \, \Omega \, A^j \, . \tag{9}$$

This implicitly defines α^j given A^j; in other words, it is principal j's best response to the choices of all the other principals. In the Nash equilibrium, such relationships must hold simultaneously for all j. Adding them over j, and recognizing that $A^j = \alpha - \alpha^j$ sum to $(n - 1) \, \alpha$ where n is the number of principals involved, we have

$$b = (I + n \, r \, C \, \Omega) \, \alpha \, . \tag{10}$$

This defines the aggregate incentive scheme in equilibrium. Bernheim and Whinston (1986) provide a more direct way of finding the aggregate scheme. The advantage of the approach here is that we can go back to (9) and find the individual principals' incentive schemes in equilibrium. I will do that in a moment, but first we can obtain some useful results from the aggregate.

Compare the second-best incentive scheme defined by (7), where all the principals are united, and the aggregate scheme (10) that emerges from the Nash equilibrium, where they are not. The two expressions are remarkably alike, except for the factor n that multiplies a term on the right-hand side. In other words, the effect of the lack of cooperation between the principals is exactly as if the risk-aversion of the agent were multiplied by a factor equal to the number of principals. Recall that the need for risk-sharing is what leads to a lower-powered scheme in the second-best as compared to the first-best. Therefore in the present "third-best" Nash equilibrium between the competing principals, the overall incentives are even less powerful than those in the second-best. Moreover, the effect is proportional to the number of principals and therefore can be quite dramatic when several of these are involved. Roughly speaking, we can say that the power of the incentive scheme becomes inversely proportional to the number of principals.

To understand the reason for this dampening of incentives, let us find an explicit expression for the equilibrium incentive scheme of an individual principal. Noting that (9) can be written

$$b^j = \alpha^j + r\, C\, \Omega\, \alpha,$$

and substituting from (10), we find

$$\alpha^j = b^j - r\, C\, \Omega\, (I + n\, r\, C\, \Omega)^{-1}\, b\,. \tag{11}$$

Consider the case where $n = m$, and principal j has direct concern only for the output of task j. Then all components of b^j except the j-th are zero, but that does not hold for α^j. The second term in (11) contributes to all the other components of α^j. In the normal case, we expect all these other components to be negative. In other words, principal j will typically penalize all other dimensions of the agent's effort. Of course this taken by itself lowers the agent's utility, but the constant term β^j in the scheme can always be adjusted to ensure that the agent gets non-negative surplus from his relationship with principal j and therefore remains willing to participate.

The point is that even though principal j is not directly concerned with any other components of output, he would like the agent to exert less effort in those dimensions because that will induce the agent to make more effort in the dimension that benefits principal j. This effect actually comes about through two avenues, which we see from a closer examination of the expression (8) for the bilateral surplus between the agent and principal j.

The first effect comes from the second term in this expression. For simplicity, suppose that only the j-th component of b^j in principal j's benefit is nonzero. (So long as the principals' interests are not perfectly aligned, that is, the vectors b^j are linearly independent, we can make this true by a change of the coordinate system.) Then the term is

$$b^j_j \sum_i \Gamma_{ji}\, \alpha^j_i\,.$$

When the agent's efforts on behalf of principals i and j are substitutes in the appropriate sense, $\Gamma_{ji} < 0$, so principal j benefits from making α_i^j negative. This is an obvious direct effect.

Another effect, less obvious and indirect, comes from the third term in the expression (8). The other principals' schemes A^j affect principal j's marginal choice through the risk-premium term, $-r\,A^{j'}\,\Omega\,\alpha^j$. Because the matrix Ω has been assumed to be diagonal, this is simply

$$-r\,\sum_i A_i^j\,\Omega_{ii}\,\alpha_i^j.$$

Let us ask if a situation where each principal chooses a scheme based only on his dimension of output can be an equilibrium. Suppose for a moment that each principal $i \neq j$ offers a positive incentive for the agent's effort in dimension i and zero incentive for other dimensions. This implies $A_j^j = 0$, and $A_i^j > 0$ for all $i \neq j$ (remember that the A^j are the vectors of coefficients summed over all the principals *except* j). Now look at principal j's best response. In the above sum, all the coefficients of α_i^j for $i \neq j$ are negative, so principal j benefits by making his own α_i^j negative. The reason is that these negative components induce the agent to work less hard for the other principals, which makes his income from them less risky. Then principal j need only pay a smaller risk premium to induce the agent to work harder at the margin on his own behalf. The same argument applies to all the principals, so the initial supposition of independence of their incentive schemes ($A_j^j = 0$) cannot remain true in equilibrium. This effect persists even when the marginal cost of the agent's effort for one principal is independent of that for others, because even when C is diagonal and therefore so is its inverse Γ, we have

$$t_i = \Gamma_{ii} \sum_j \alpha_i^j .$$

Of course when the agent's cost of effort is not separable, the matrix Γ has off-diagonal terms, and the other principals' interests affect the bilateral surplus through the more direct effect that was discussed earlier.

Such conditioning of each principal's incentives on the outcomes of direct interest to the other principals has repercussions for the Nash equilibrium. If principal j increases the j-th component of his α^j, the agent will increase t_j, the j-th component of effort. This raises the expected value of x_j, the j-th component of output, and therefore the agent's receipt from principal j. But the other principals k have negative j-th coefficients of their incentive parameters α^k, so the agent's payment to them increases as well. In other words, some of principal j's money passes to the other principals via the agent. This leakage is not complete, because as (9) shows, the reaction functions do not have slope -1; but it is significant. For principal j, the leakage to other principals makes it much less desirable to offer a powerful incentive scheme. That is why the equilibrium ends up with substantially lower-powered aggregate incentives.

Effect of Restrictions on Principals

If all the principals could get together and make a binding agreement to offer a jointly agreed-upon incentive scheme and divide up the proceeds with suitable transfer payments among themselves, they could achieve the second-best.

However, the necessary ongoing cooperation may not be possible in the political context, and each principal has an incentive to cheat on the agreement and offer a scheme that gets him some extra benefit. In such a situation, a constitutional provision that limits such cheating, if enforceable, can be mutually beneficial. We have seen that the problem is each principal's provision of a negative marginal incentive for the agent's effort on behalf of the other principals. Therefore it may be desirable to have a constitutional rule that prevents such actions. This can be done either by restricting observation so that each principal cannot see the dimensions of the outcome that pertain to other principals, or by forbidding action based on such other dimensions even when they are observable. Let us examine the consequences of this.

For this, consider the case where $n = m$, and each principal j benefits from only the j-th component of output, so $b_k^j = 0$ for all $k \neq j$. We also restrict every vector α^j to have zero coefficients α_k^j for all $k \neq j$. Then the expression (8) for the bilateral surplus between the j-th principal and the agent becomes

$$b^{j'} \Gamma A^j + b_j^j \Gamma_{jj} \alpha_j^j - \tfrac{1}{2} (\Gamma_{jj} + r \, \Omega_{jj}) (\alpha_j^j)^2 . \tag{12}$$

Choosing α_j^j to maximize this gives the first-order condition

$$\Gamma_{jj} \, b_j^j = (\Gamma_{jj} + r \, \Omega_{jj}) \alpha_j^j . \tag{13}$$

The Nash equilibrium of the principals' interaction with their constrained choices is defined by these equations for all j.

Note that the number of principals no longer multiplies the agent's risk-aversion; thus that major source of weakness of incentives is missing. In fact, the incentives in this equilibrium can be more powerful than those in the second-best. The reason is that each principal must now use a positive coefficient on the component of output that is of direct concern to him in order to divert the agent from tasks that benefit the other principals. This competition among the principals leads them to raise those coefficients to higher levels.

The effect is seen most dramatically in the limiting case where the different components of effort become perfect substitutes in the agent's utility function. Then the determinant of C goes to zero, and all entries in the inverse matrix Γ go to infinity. Using this in (13) above, we have

$$\alpha_j^j = b_j^j \text{ for all } j, \text{ or } \alpha = b.$$

The resulting aggregate incentive scheme reproduces the first-best! More generally, if different components of the effort are close substitutes, then the constrained Nash equilibrium is better than the second-best. Instead of uniting the principals, society as a whole does better to force each to compete fiercely using positive incentive for matters of direct concern to him, but prohibit them from competing by using negative incentives for matters of concern to others.

References

Aranson, Peter H., and Peter C. Ordeshook. 1981. "Alternative Theories of the Growth of Government and Their Implications for Constitutional Tax and Spending Limits." In *Tax and Expenditure Limitations*, eds. Helen F. Ladd and T. Nicolaus Tideman. Washington, DC: Urban Institute, pp. 143–176.

Armstrong, Mark, Simon Cowan, and John Vickers. 1994. *Regulatory Reform: Economic Analysis and British Experience*. Cambridge, MA: MIT Press.

Arnold, R. Douglas. 1990. *The Logic of Congressional Action*. New Haven, CT: Yale University Press.

Arnott, Richard, and Joseph E. Stiglitz. 1989. "The Welfare Economics of Moral Hazard." In *Risk, Information and Insurance: Essays in the Memory of Karl H. Borch*, ed. Henri Louberge. Norwell, MA: Kluwer Academic Publishers, pp. 91–122.

Arthur, W. Brian. 1994. *Increasing Returns and Path Dependence in the Economy*. Ann Arbor, MI: University of Michigan Press.

Bagwell, Kyle, and Robert W. Staiger. 1990. "A Theory of Managed Trade." *American Economic Review* 80, no. 4: 779–795.

Baldwin, Robert E. 1988. "The Economics of the GATT." In *Trade Policy in a Changing World Economy*, ed. Robert E. Baldwin. Chicago, IL: University of Chicago Press, pp. 137–147.

Banks, Jeffrey S. 1991. *Signaling Games in Political Science*. Reading, U.K.: Harwood Academic Publishers.

Baron, David, and Roger Myerson. 1982. "Regulating a Monopolist with Unknown Costs." *Econometrica* 50, no. 4: 911–930.

Barzel, Yoram. 1989. *Economic Analysis of Property Rights.* New York: Cambridge University Press.

Becker, Gary W. 1983. "A Theory of Competition among Pressure Groups for Political Influence." *Quarterly Journal of Economics* 98, no. 3: 371–400.

Bernheim, B. Douglas, and Michael Whinston. 1986. "Common Agency." *Econometrica* 54, no. 4: 911–930.

Besley, Timothy, and Stephen Coate. 1994. "An Economic Model of Representative Democracy." Working paper, Princeton University; December.

Besley, Timothy, and Stephen Coate. 1995. "Efficient Policy Choice in a Representative Democracy: A Dynamic Analysis." Working paper, Princeton University; May.

Bhagwati, Jagdish N. 1992. *The World Trading System at Risk.* Princeton, NJ: Princeton University Press.

Billingsley, Patrick. 1986. *Probability and Measure.* 2d ed. New York: John Wiley.

Blinder, Alan S. 1987. *Hard Heads, Soft Hearts.* Reading, MA: Addison-Wesley.

Blinder, Alan S., and Douglas Holtz-Eakin. 1984. "Public Opinion and the Balanced Budget." *American Economic Review* 74, no. 2 (Papers and Proceedings): 144–149.

Buchanan, James M. 1973. "The Coase Theorem and the Theory of the State." *Natural Resources Journal*, 13, no. 4: 579–594.

Buchanan, James M. 1975. "A Contractarian Paradigm for Applying Economic Theory," *American Economic Review*, 65, no. 2 (Papers and Proceedings): 225–230.

Buchanan, James M. 1987. "The Constitution of Economic Policy." *American Economic Review* 77, no. 3: 243–250.

Buchanan, James M. 1988. "Contractarian Political Economy and Constitutional Interpretation." *American Economic Review* 78, no. 2 (Papers and Proceedings): 135–139.

Buchanan, James M., and Gordon Tullock. 1962. *The Calculus of Consent*, Ann Arbor, MI: University of Michigan Press.

Bulow, Jeremy, and Kenneth Rogoff. 1989. "Sovereign Debt: Is to Forgive to Forget?" *American Economic Review* 79, no. 1: 43–50.

Butler, David, Andrew Adonis, and Tony Travers. 1994. *Failure in British Government: The Politics of the Poll Tax.* Oxford, U.K.: Oxford University Press.

Cassing, James H., and Arye L. Hillman. 1986. "Shifting Comparative Advantage and Senescent Industry Collapse." *American Economic Review* 76, no. 3: 516–523.

Clarke, Edward H. 1971. "Multipart Pricing of Public Goods." *Public Choice* 11 (fall): 17–33.

Cogan, John F. 1994. "The Dispersion of Spending Authority and Federal Budget Deficits." In Cogan et al., op cit., pp. 16–40.

Cogan, John F., Timothy J. Muris, and Allen Schick. 1994. *The Budget Puzzle: Understanding Federal Spending.* Stanford, CA: Stanford University Press.

Collins, Susan M., and Barry P. Bosworth, eds. 1994. *The New GATT: Implications for the United States.* Washington, DC: Brookings.

Dam, Kenneth W. 1970. *The GATT: International Law and Economic Organization.* Chicago, IL: University of Chicago Press.

David, Paul. 1985. "Clio and the Economics of QWERTY." *American Economic Review* 75, no. 2 (Papers and Proceedings): 332–337.

Davis, Douglas D., and Charles A. Holt. 1993. *Experimental Economics.* Princeton, NJ: Princeton University Press.

Demsetz, Harold. 1964. "The Exchange and Enforcement of Property Rights." *Journal of Law and Economics* 7: 11–26.

Destler, I. M. 1992. *American Trade Politics.* 2d ed. Washington, DC: Institute for International Economics.

Dewatripont, Mathias, and Jean Tirole. 1995. "Advocates." Working paper, ECARE, Institut d'Etudes Européennes, Brussells, April.

Diamond, Peter A. 1994. "Theory and Policy." Paper presented at the World Bank Social Safety Nets Seminar, November 7.

Diebold, William. 1952. *The End of the I.T.O.* Princeton University, International Finance Section: Essays in International Finance, no. 16, October.

Dixit, Avinash. 1987. "Strategic Aspects of Trade Policy." In *Advances in Economic Theory: Fifth World Congress,* ed. Truman Bewley. Cambridge, U.K.: Cambridge University Press, pp. 329–362.

Dixit, Avinash. 1995. "Stochastic Dynamic Investment and Employment Decisions." Working paper, Princeton University.

Dixit, Avinash, and John Londregan. 1995. "Redistributive Politics and Economic Efficiency." *American Political Science Review* 89, no. 4: 856–866.

Dixit, Avinash, and John Londregan. 1996. "The Determinants of Success of Special Interests in Redistributive Politics." *Journal of Politics* forthcoming.

Dixit, Avinash, and Barry Nalebuff. 1991. *Thinking Strategically: The Competitive Edge in Business, Politics, and Everyday Life.* New York: Norton.

Eizenstat, Stuart E. 1992 "Economists and White House Decisions." *Journal of Economic Perspectives* 6, no. 3: 65–72.

Epstein, David, and Sharyn O'Halloran. 1994. "Common Agency and Representation." Working paper, Columbia University, April.

Evans, Philip, and James Walsh. 1994. *The EIU Guide to the New GATT.* London: Economist Intelligence Unit.

Ferejohn, John. 1986. "Incumbent Performance and Electoral Control." *Public Choice* 50, no. 1: 5–26.

Fudenberg, Drew, and Jean Tirole. 1991. *Game Theory.* Cambridge, MA: MIT Press.

Gilligan, Thomas W., and Keith Krehbiel. 1987, "Collective Decisionmaking and Standing Committees: An Informational Rationale for Restrictive Amendment Procedures." *Journal of Law, Economics, and Organization* 3, no. 2: 287–335.

Gould, Stephen Jay. 1980. *The Panda's Thumb*. New York: Norton.

Gould, Stephen Jay. 1985. *The Flamingo's Smile*, New York: Norton.

Greenwald, Bruce, and Joseph E. Stiglitz. 1986. "Externalities in Economies with Imperfect Information and Incomplete Markets." *Quarterly Journal of Economics* 101, no. 2: 229–264.

Greif, Avner. 1993. "Contract Enforceability and Economic Institutions in Early Trade: The Maghribi Traders' Coalition." *American Economic Review* 83, no. 3: 525–548.

Grossman, Gene M., and Elhanan Helpman. 1994. "Protection for Sale." *American Economic Review*, 84, no. 4: 833–850.

Groves, Theodore, and John Ledyard. 1977. "Optimal Allocation of Public Goods: A Solution to the 'Free Rider' Problem." *Econometrica* 45, no. 4: 783–809.

Guesnerie, Roger. 1995. *A Contribution to the Pure Theory of Taxation*. Econometric Society Monograph no. 25, Cambridge, U.K.: Cambridge University Press.

Hamilton, Lee H. 1992. "Economists as Public Policy Advisers." *Journal of Economic Perspectives*, 6, no. 3: 61–64.

Harsanyi, John C. 1953. "Cardinal Utility in Welfare Economics and the Theory of Risk-Taking." *Journal of Political Economy* 61, no. 5: 434–435.

Hathaway, Dale E. 1987. *Agriculture and the GATT: Writing the Rules*. Washington, DC: Institute for International Economics.

Haubrich, Joseph G. and Joseph A. Ritter. 1995. "Commitment as Irreversible Investment." Working paper no. 95–004, Federal Reserve Bank of St. Louis, March.

Hillman, Arye L. 1989. *The Political Economy of Protection*. Reading, U.K.: Harwood Academic Publishers.

Holmström, Bengt, and Paul Milgrom. 1987. "Aggregation and Linearity in the Provision of Intertemporal Incentives." *Econometrica* 55, no. 2: 303–328.

Holmström, Bengt and Paul Milgrom. 1988. "Common Agency and Exclusive Dealing." Working paper, Yale University, School of Management.

Holmström, Bengt, and Paul Milgrom. 1990. "Regulating Trade Among Agents." *Journal of Institutional and Theoretical Economics* 146, no. 1: 85–105.

Holmström, Bengt, and Paul Milgrom. 1991. "Multitask Principal-Agent Analysis: Incentive Contracts, Asset Ownership, and Job Design." *Journal of Law, Economics, and Organization* 7, Special Issue: 24–51.

Hudec, Robert E. 1990. *The GATT Legal System and World Trade Diplomacy.* 2d ed. Salem, NH: Butterworths.

Hudec, Robert E. 1993. *Enforcing International Trade Law: The Evolution of the Modern GATT Legal System.* Salem, NH: Butterworths.

Hufbauer, Gary C., Diane T. Berliner, and Kimberly A. Elliott. 1986. *Trade Protection in the United States: 31 Case Studies.* Washington, DC: Institute for International Economics.

Hufbauer, Gary C., and Kimberly A. Elliott. 1994. *Measuring the Costs of Protection in the United States.* Washington, DC: Institute for International Economics.

Jackson, John H. 1989. *The World Trading System: Law and Policy of International Economic Relations.* Cambridge, MA: MIT Press.

Jackson, John H. 1990. *Restructuring the GATT System.* New York: Council on Foreign Relations.

Joskow, Paul L., and Roger C. Noll. 1981. "Regulation in Theory and Practice: An Overview." In *Studies in Public Regulation*, ed. G. Fromm. Cambridge, MA: MIT Press, pp. 1–65.

Joskow, Paul L., and Richard Schmalensee. 1986. "Incentive Regulation for Electric Utilities." *Yale Journal on Regulation*, 4, no. 1: 1–49.

Journal of Economic Perspectives. 1987. Symposium on Tax Reform, 1, no. 1 (Summer).

Katzenstein, Peter J. 1985. *Small States in World Markets.* Ithaca, NY: Cornell University Press.

Kosters, Marvin H., ed. 1992. *Fiscal Politics and the Budget Enforcement Act.* Washington, DC: AEI Press.

Kotlikoff, Laurence J. 1992. *Generational Accounting.* New York: Free Press.

Krishna, Kala. 1989. "Trade Restrictions as Facilitating Practices." *Journal of International Economics* 26, Nos.3–4: 251–270.

Krueger, Anne O. 1990. "The Political Economy of Controls: American Sugar." In *Public Policy and Economic Development,* eds. Maurice Scott and Deepak Lal. Oxford, U.K.: Clarendon Press.

Krugman, Paul R. 1987. "Is Free Trade Passé?" *Journal of Economic Perspectives* 1, no. 2: 131–144.

Krugman, Paul R. 1990. *The Age of Diminished Expectations.* Cambridge, MA: MIT Press.

Krugman, Paul R. 1994. "The Fall and Rise of Development Economics." In *Rethinking the Development Experience,* eds. Lloyd Rodwin and Donald A. Schön. Washington, DC: Brookings, pp. 39–58.

Kydland, Finn S., and Edward C. Prescott. 1977. "Rules Rather Than Discretion: The Inconsistency of Optimal Plans." *Journal of Political Economy* 85, no. 3: 473–490.

Laffont, Jean-Jacques. 1995. "Industrial Policy and Politics." Institut de France, Toulouse, manuscript.

Laffont, Jean-Jacques, and Jean Tirole. 1993. *A Theory of Incentives in Procurement and Regulation.* Cambridge, MA: MIT Press.

Levy, Brian, and Pablo T. Spiller. 1994. "The Institutional Foundations of Regulatory Commitment: A Comparative Analysis of Telecommunications Regulation." *Journal of Law, Economics, and Organization,* 10, no. 2: 201–246.

Lindbeck, Assar, Per Molander, Torsten Persson, Olof Petersson, Agnar Sandmo, Birgitta Swedenborg, and Niels Thygesen. 1994. *Turning Sweden Around.* Cambridge, MA: MIT Press.

Lindbeck, Assar, and Jörgen W. Weibull. 1987. "Balanced-Budget Redistribution as the Outcome of Political Competition." *Public Choice* 52, no. 3: 273–297.

Lohmann, Susanne. 1992. "The Optimal Degree of Commitment: Credibility versus Flexibility." *American Economic Review* 83, no. 1: 273–286.

Lucas, Robert E., Jr. 1990. "Supply-Side Economics: An Analytical Review." *Oxford Economic Papers* 42: 293–316.

Maggi, Giovanni. 1993. "The Role of Multilateral Institutions in International Trade Cooperation." Working paper, Stanford University, November.

Marks, Stephen V. 1993. "A Reassessment of the Empirical Evidence on the U.S. Sugar Program." In *The Economics and Politics of World Sugar Policies,* eds. Stephen V. Marks and Keith E. Maskus. Ann Arbor, MI: University of Michigan Press, pp. 79–108.

Martimort, David. 1992. "Multi-Principaux avec Anti-Selection." *Annales D'Économie et de Statistique,* No. 28, pp. 1–37.

Martimort, David. 1995. "Exclusive Dealing, Common Agency, and Multiprincipals Incentive Theory." Working paper, IDEI, Université des Sciences Sociales, Toulouse.

McCubbins, Matthew D., Roger G. Noll, and Barry R. Weingast. 1987. "Administrative Procedures as Instruments of Political Control." *Journal of Law, Economics, and Organization* 3, no. 2: 242–77.

McGuire, Martin C., and Mancur Olson. 1995. "The Economics of Autocracy and Majority Rule." Working paper, IRIS Center, University of Maryland.

McMillan, John. 1994. "Selling Spectrum Rights." *Journal of Economic Perspectives* 8, no. 3: 145–162.

Mirrlees, James A. 1971. "An Exploration in the Theory of Optimal Income Taxation." *Review of Economic Studies* 38, no. 2: 175–208.

Moe, Terry M. 1990. "The Politics of Structural Choice: Toward a Theory of Public Bureaucracy." In *Organization Theory*, ed. Oliver E. Williamson. New York: Oxford University Press, pp. 116–153.

Moser, Peter. 1990. *The Political Economy of the GATT.* Grüsch, Switzerland: Verlag Rüegger.

Mueller, Dennis C. 1989. *Public Choice II.* Cambridge, U.K.: Cambridge University Press.

Muris, Timothy J. 1994. "The Uses and Abuses of Budget Baselines." In Cogan et al., op. cit., pp. 41–78.

Musgrave, Richard A. 1959. *The Theory of Public Finance.* New York: McGraw-Hill.

Myerson, Roger. 1979. "Incentive Compatibility and the Bargaining Problem." *Econometrica* 47, no. 1: 61–73.

Niskanen, William A. 1992. "The Case for a New Fiscal Constitution." *Journal of Economic Perspectives* 6, no. 2: 13–24.

Noll, Roger G. 1989. "Economic Perspectives on the Politics of Regulation." In *Handbook of Industrial Organization, Volume II,* eds. Richard Schmalensee and Robert Willig. Amsterdam: North-Holland, pp. 1253–1287.

Nordhaus, William. 1975. "The Political Business Cycle." *Review of Economic Studies* 42, no. 2: 169–190.

North, Douglass C. 1990a. *Institutions, Institutional Change, and Economic Performance.* New York: Cambridge University Press.

North, Douglass C. 1990b. "A Transaction Cost Theory of Politics." *Journal of Theoretical Politics* 2, no. 4: 355–367.

North, Douglass C. 1994. "Economic Performance Through Time." *American Economic Review* 84, no. 3: 359–368.

Olson, Mancur. 1965. *The Logic of Collective Action.* Cambridge, MA: Harvard University Press.

Olson, Mancur. 1993. "Dictatorship, Democracy, and Development." *American Political Science Review* 87, no. 3: 567–576.

Ordeshook, Peter C. 1990. "The Emerging Discipline of Political Economy." In *Perspectives on Positive Political Economy*. eds. James E. Alt and Kenneth A. Shepsle. New York: Cambridge University Press, pp. 9–30.

Penner, Rudolph. 1992. "Political Economics of the 1990 Budget Agreement." In Kosters, ed., op. cit., pp. 1–19.

Persson, Mats, Torsten Persson, and Lars E. O. Svensson. 1987. "Time Consistency of Fiscal and Monetary Policy." *Econometrica* 55, no. 6: 1419–1431.

Persson, Torsten and Guido Tabellini. 1990. *Macroeconomic Policy, Credibility and Politics*. Reading, U.K.: Harwood Academic Publishers.

Persson, Torsten, and Guido Tabellini, eds. 1994a. *Monetary and Fiscal Policy: Volume I: Credibility*. Cambridge, MA: MIT Press.

Persson, Torsten, and Guido Tabellini eds. 1994b. *Monetary and Fiscal Policy: Volume II: Politics*. Cambridge, MA: MIT Press.

Rawls, John. 1971. *A Theory of Justice*, Cambridge, MA: Harvard University Press.

Rogoff, Kenneth S. 1985. "The Optimal Degree of Commitment to an Intermediate Monetary Target." *Quarterly Journal of Economics* 100, no. 4: 1169–1190.

Rogoff, Kenneth S. 1990. "Equilibrium Political Budget Cycles." *American Economic Review* 80, no. 1: 21–36.

Roth, Alvin. 1984. "The Evolution of the Labor Market for Medical Interns and Residents: A Case Study in Game Theory." *Journal of Political Economy* 92, no. 6: 991–1016.

Roth, Alvin, and Marilda A. Sotomayor. 1990, *Two-Sided Matching*. New York: Cambridge University Press.

Russell, Bertrand. 1945. *A History of Western Philosophy*. New York: Simon and Schuster.

Sandmo, Agnar. 1991. "Economists and the Welfare State." *European Economic Review* 35, Nos. 2–3: 213–239.

Schelling, Thomas C. 1960. *The Strategy of Conflict.* Cambridge, MA: Harvard University Press.

Schick, Allen. 1992. "Deficit Budgeting in the Age of Divided Government." In Kosters, ed., op. cit., pp. 20–36.

Schultze, Charles L. 1992. "Is There a Bias Toward Excess in the U.S. Government Budgets or Deficits?" *Journal of Economic Perspectives* 6, no. 2: 25–43.

Shapley, Lloyd S., and Martin Shubik. 1969. "On the Core of Economic Systems with Externalities." *American Economic Review* 59, no. 4: 678–684.

Shepsle, Kenneth A. 1991. "Models of Multiparty Electoral Competition," Reading, U.K.: Harwood Academic Publishers.

Shepsle, Kenneth A. and Barry R. Weingast. 1981. "Political Preference for the Pork Barrel: A Generalization." *American Journal of Political Science* 25, no. 1: 96–111.

Sinn, Hans-Werner. 1988. "United States Tax Reform 1981 and 1986: Impact on International Capital Markets and Capital Flows." *National Tax Journal* 41, no. 3: 327–340.

Sinn, Hans-Werner. 1993. "Pigou and Clarke Join Hands." *Public Choice* 78, no. 1: 79–91.

Snape, Richard H. ed. 1986. *Issues in World Trade Policy—GATT at the Crossroads.* Basingstoke, U.K.: Macmillan.

Spiller, Pablo T. 1990. "Politicians, Interest Groups, and Regulators." *Journal of Law and Economics* 23, no. 1: 65–101.

Staiger, Robert W. 1995. "International Rules and Institutions for Trade Policy." In *Handbook of International Economics, Volume III,* eds. Gene M. Grossman and Kenneth Rogoff. Amsterdam: North-Holland.

Stiglitz, Joseph E. 1994. *Whither Socialism?* Cambridge, MA: MIT Press.

Stiglitz, Joseph E. et al. 1989. *The Economic Role of the State.* Oxford, U.K.: Basil Blackwell.

Stole, Lars. 1990. "Mechanism Design Under Common Agency." Working paper, MIT, Cambridge, MA.

Thurow, Lester C. 1992. *Head to Head: The Coming Economic Battle Among Japan, Europe and America.* New York: Morrow.

Tirole, Jean. 1994. "The Internal Organization of Government." *Oxford Economic Papers* 46, no. 1: 1–29.

Varian, Hal R. 1994. "A Solution to the Problem of Externalities When Agents Are Well-Informed." *American Economic Review* 84, no. 5: 1278–1293.

Vickrey, William. 1961. "Counterspeculation, Auctions and Competitive Sealed Tenders." *Journal of Finance*, 16, no. 1: 8–37.

Wicksell, Knut. 1896. *Finanztheoretische Untersuchungen.* Jena: Gustav Fisher.

Wildavsky, Aaron. 1984. *The Politics of the Budgetary Process.* 4th ed. Boston, MA: Little, Brown.

Williamson, Oliver E. 1985. *The Economic Institutions of Capitalism.* New York: Free Press.

Williamson, Oliver E. 1989. "Transaction Cost Economics." In *Handbook of Industrial Organization, Volume I,* eds. Richard Schmalensee and Robert Willig. Amsterdam: North-Holland, pp. 135–182.

Williamson, Oliver E. 1996. "The Politics and Economics of Redistribution and Efficiency." In *The Mechanisms of Governance*, Oxford, U.K.: Oxford University Press.

Wilson, James Q. 1989. *Bureaucracy: What Government Agencies Do and Why They Do It.* New York: Basic Books.

Yoffie, David B., and Benjamin Gomes-Casseres. 1994. *International Trade and Competition.* New York: McGraw-Hill.

Name Index

Subject Index